WHAT ARE LITTLE GIRLS MADE OF ?

WHAT ARE LITTLE GIRLS MADE OF ?

A GUIDE TO FEMALE
ROLE MODELS IN
CHILDREN'S BOOKS

Marjorie N. Allen

☑® Facts On File, Inc.

Library of Congress Cataloging-in-Publication Data

Allen, Marjorie N.
    What are little girls made of? : A guide to female role models in children's books / by Marjorie N. Allen.
        p. cm.
    Includes bibliographical references and index.
    ISBN 0-8160-3673-X
    1. Children's stories, American—History and criticism.   2. Girls in literature.
3. Children's stories, American—Women authors—History and criticism.   4. Children's stories, English—History and criticism.   5. Girls—United States—Books and reading.
6. Authorship—Sex differences.   7. Women in literature.   8. Role models. I. Title.
PS374.G55A55 1998
810.9'9282—dc21   98-8148

Text design by Evelyn Horovicz
Cover design by Semadar Megged

Printed in the United States of America

MP FOF 10 9 8 7 6 5 4 3 2 1

This book is printed on acid-free paper.

In memory of my mother, Lauretta Nicholson, who had so much more to give.

Grateful acknowledgment is made to the following for permission to reproduce illustrations.

Luann comic strip copyright ©December 8, 1996, GEC Inc. by Greg Evans. Reprinted by permission of Greg Evans. Distributed by United Feature Syndicate Inc.

Illustration by Elise Primavera, from *Christina Katerina and the Time She Quit the Family* by Patricia Lee Gauch. Illustration copyright ©1987 by Elise Primavera. Reprinted by permission of G.P. Putnam's Sons.

Cover, from *Mandy* by Barbara Booth. Jacket illustration copyright ©1991 by Jim LaMarche. Reprinted by permission of Lothrop, Lee and Shepard Books, a division of William Morrow and Company Inc.

Cover, from *The Midwife's Apprentice* by Karen Cushman. Jacket illustration copyright ©1995 by Trina Schart Hyman. Reprinted by permission of Clarion Books/Houghton Mifflin Company. All rights reserved.

Jacket cover, from *Beyond the Burning Time* by Kathryn Lasky, illustration by David Shannon. Jacket copyright ©1994 by David Shannon. Reprinted by permission of Scholastic Inc.

Illustration by Marc Simont, from *In the Year of the Boar and Jackie Robinson* by Bette Bao Lord. Copyright©1984 by Marc Simont. Used by permission of HarperCollins Publishers.

Cover, from *The Last Rainmaker* by Sherry Garland. Cover illustration copyright ©1997 by Tracy Sabin. Jacket design by Lisa Peters. Reprinted by permission of Tracy Sabin and Harcourt Brace & Co. All rights reserved.

Illustration by John Palencar, from *Arilla Sun Down* by Virginia Hamilton. Illustration copyright ©1995 by Scholastic Inc. Reproduced by permission. POINT is a registered trademark of Scholastic Inc.

Illustration, from *Harriet the Spy* by Louise Fitzhugh. Copyright ©1964 by Louise Fitzhugh. Used by permission of HarperCollins Publishers. This selection may not be re-illustrated.

Illustration, from *Daphne Eloise Slater, Who's Tall for Her Age* by Gina Willner-Pardo. Illustration copyright ©1997 by Glo Coalson. Reprinted by permission of Clarion Books/Houghton Mifflin Company. All rights reserved.

If we are to set women to the same tasks as men,

we must teach them the same things.

They must have the same two branches of training

for mind and body and also be taught the art of

war, and they must receive the same treatment.

—Plato, *The Republic*

CONTENTS

ACKNOWLEDGMENTS

When I was accepted into the Ada Comstock Program at Smith College, I was already past 50. It was inevitable at a women's college that I would decide to take some courses in feminist theory, and it was equally inevitable that I would sometimes upset the young women in my class by making statements that reflected my ignorance of the feminist movement. Even so, I am and always have been a firm believer in equal rights for women and equal respect for women's accomplishments. In my four years at Smith, I learned a great deal about the value of being female, about self-confidence, and about perseverance. I graduated with the conviction that I could be anything I wanted to be and do anything I wanted to do. I am forever grateful to Eleanor Rothman and the Ada Comstock Scholars' Program at Smith for giving me the opportunity to enroll.

I also would like to thank my editors at Facts On File, Hilary Poole and Anne Savarese, whose enthusiasm and astute editing guided me through the writing of this book; my agent, Deborah Schneider, who, as usual, did all the right things for me; and my own private copy editor and good friend, Judy Storie. Finally, I would also like to acknowledge members of the Prodigy Books & Writing Bulletin Board and America Online, as well as participants in various Internet newsgroups, who responded to my on-line requests by offering their comments regarding children's literature and female identity.

WHAT ARE LITTLE GIRLS MADE OF?

INTRODUCTION:
DEFINING SELF

Only 29 percent of high
school girls are happy with
themselves compared to 46
percent of boys.

—Patricia Aburdene
and John Naisbitt, *Megatrends for
Women: From Liberation to Leadership*

I'm Nobody! Who are you?

Are you—Nobody—too?

Then there's the pair of us!

Don't tell! they'd advertise—you know!

—Emily Dickinson

Parents have a strong influence on their children in the early years of development, but by the time a child begins to interact with other children, around the age of two, the bid for independence and individuality begins. Gradually, even before school age, the child looks outside the family for role models, and the influence of peers and mass media in this age of pervasive communication greatly increases. Sociological studies indicate that although parents are responsible for the socialization of children, the influence of peers and mass media has assumed a much larger role in a child's social identity in the last few decades.[1]

Once upon a time, role models were public figures who exhibited virtues that parents hoped their children might emulate: strength, fair play, bravery, confidence, compassion, respect, and honesty. These role models usually were male.

Today, public figures have been dissected into oblivion by the media. Sports heroes gamble and take drugs. Presidents don't always tell the truth. Entertainers have feet of clay. The pedestals have toppled, and young people are hard pressed to find anyone to meet their expectations. Despite the popular lament that there are no more heroes, however, heroes continue to exist in books for children—heroes both male *and* female.

Many factors influence children as they grow and develop, especially the books they read and have read to them. These stories influence the way they see the world and one another. In the early 1980s educators Kenneth Goodman and Lucy McCormick Calkins

This particular Luann *comic strip by Greg Evans represents the biased images of men and women promoted by advertisers.*

introduced the whole-language movement into the schools, a philosophy that called for connecting print with meaning by reading books and discussing them in the classroom. Teachers were introduced to children's books in which story and characters took precedence over vocabulary and spelling lists. This new philosophy appealed to teachers who were beginning to question the value of basal readers and were looking for a way to make reading and writing more appealing to their students. In the past several years, many schools have replaced basal readers with a literature-based curriculum, and the market demand for children's books has escalated.[2]

Because books are so much a part of a child's upbringing, especially with literature-based curricula in the schools, parents need to know what books their children are reading and how discussion of those books might lead to a more positive identity. Such books abound from both the past—for example, L. Frank Baum's *The*

I read the Cherry Ames student nurse books. In every book Cherry would meet a new young doctor and have an innocent romance in a glorious setting. Thank goodness I also read Nancy Drew and the Dana sisters' mysteries. Those amateur sleuths were competent and confident, brave and adventurous.

— Mary Pipher, *Reviving Ophelia: Saving the Selves of Adolescent Girls*

Wonderful Wizard of Oz (1900) in which a conventional and practical Dorothy bravely leads a group of males on a quest—and the present—for example, *Weetzie Bat* (1991) by Francesca Lia Block in which an unconventional young woman is determined to find her way in a chaotic Los Angeles society. A contemporary concern among parents and educators is that far too many adolescents lack self-esteem. The question is why—and why this problem affects more girls than boys.

WOMEN AND SOCIETY

In adult literature, the women who carved places for themselves did so through development of their talents and sheer perseverance against great odds. Most of them never knew how influential they would become, how much dialogue their works would generate among their readers. Their influence paved the way for contemporary women writers and editors to gain recognition in children's literature, an area that only recently has begun to interest critics and historians. Without the efforts of such women as Jane Austen, Emily Dickinson, Edith Wharton, and Virginia Woolf, women writers, including those in the children's literature field, might never have become a major influence in 20th-century society, and the wide variety of female heroes in children's books might never have come into being.

Ursula K. Le Guin once wrote, "An adult . . . is a child who survived." Perhaps, for purposes of this book, the quote might read: An adult woman is a girl who has survived adolescence. Little girls, before they reach puberty can be courageous, competent, and irreverent; they can be nurturing, compassionate, and introspective. They're not yet constrained by gender-role expectations. Clinical psychologist Mary Pipher notes that "almost all the heroines of girls' literature come from this age group—Anne of Green Gables, Heidi, Pippi Longstocking, and Caddie Woodlawn."[3]

When a baby is born, people immediately want to know whether it's a boy or a girl, as if gender can predetermine the future of the child. During much of the 20th century, it was a woman's fate either to marry and merge her identity with her husband's or to be considered a spinster—in other words, a failure. Even some of the most notable women in literature were considered failures when they didn't marry. In the last decades of the century, a woman has more choices. She can now marry and keep her family name if she wishes, or take her husband's name, or remain single and not be ostracized. Whatever her choice, she can set individual goals and maintain her own identity. The barriers are tumbling—in sports, in business, and in politics.

As a result, it's important for all of today's young people—both male and female—to be aware of the wide spectrum of opportunities available to them. Women no longer have to set aside career goals until child rearing is complete. In some homes, child rearing has become a shared responsibility, with the father also acting as nurturer. In this electronic age, one parent might be working at home. Day care centers and extended families supplement caretaking. No longer is a woman expected to sacrifice self for husband and family.

We haven't created a society quite like the one depicted in Ursula K. Le Guin's *The Left Hand of Darkness* (1969), where *kemmering* (a temporary development of sexual identity for the purpose of propagation) allows for an androgynous society the majority of the time. In the setting of Le Guin's novel, the role of "mother" as we know it doesn't exist. But some questions for the 21st century arise: How will society define the roles of male and female? How can parents prepare their daughters and sons to be confident and assertive, yet compassionate and caring, and able to share common goals? Such an effort is important in a society in which only 29 percent of high school girls and 46 percent of high school boys are happy with themselves.[4]

BALANCING THE SCALES

The struggle for women to gain equal standing in society has been a slow process in a world that strives for dominance rather than balance and integration. In 1894 American suffragist Susan B. Anthony noted in a speech that although younger women might take their freedoms for granted, every inch of ground a woman "stands upon today has been gained by the hard work of some little handful of women of the past." In 1820, when Anthony was born, a married woman in America had no legal rights within the marriage. Women could not own property, attend college, or vote.[5]

In the 1920s, once women had obtained the right to vote, the women's movement declined and didn't really begin to move again until the 1960s. Thanks to the efforts of dedicated men and women, however, the '20s became the premier decade of children's books in America. It was a time of experimentation in education, when children were in the public eye. Bertha Mahony, whose Bookshop for Boys and Girls opened in Boston in 1916, made children's books available to the general public and in 1924 established *The Horn Book* magazine, which to this day is "devoted exclusively to books of interest to children."[6]

Louise Seaman headed the first children's book department in a publishing house, which was established at Macmillan in 1919. Librarian Ann Carroll Moore's "Three Owls," a children's book review column, was appearing in the *New York Herald Tribune*, and by 1930, Ann Eaton was reviewing children's books in the *New York Times*. Discerning editors such as May Massee, Virginia Kirkus, and Ursula Nordstrom were developing the genre. By 1941, Nordstrom had increased her staff at Harper Brothers from 3 to 25 and over the next 25 years increased annual sales of children's books at Harper from a few hundred thousand to 10 million dollars. By the 1950s, mainly through the efforts of such women, the children's book industry had achieved the status of "big business."[7]

In 1921 a special committee of children's librarians was formed under the auspices of Frederic G. Melcher, a midwestern bookseller, to select the most distinguished contribution to American literature for children. Since then, the Newbery Medal has been presented each year for excellence in writing.[8] In 1937, the Caldecott Medal

There is no such thing as a children's book. There are books of many kinds and some of them children read.

—Pamela Travers, *The Horn Book* magazine, June 1968

was established to honor the most distinguished picture-book illustrator of the year.[9] Although the Newbery Medal was first presented in 1922, no woman received the award until 1930. Rachel Field, author of *Hitty, Her First Hundred Years* (1929), was the first female Newbery Medal winner. Her book was illustrated by Dorothy P. Lathrop, who was awarded the first Caldecott Medal, in 1938, for *Animals of the Bible* (1937).

In the field of children's literature, although all award-winning authors in the 1920s were men, in the 1930s all were women; there is no evidence of real gender bias in recognizing the creators of children's books. By the 1940s, an award-winning author or illustrator was just as apt to be a woman as a man. It is a credit to the librarians on the award committees that the quality of the work has always transcended gender consideration.

BENEFITS OF READING

So many factors are involved in shaping identity that the effect of children's books on the female psyche can be considered only a small portion of overall influence on today's children. Parents who are familiar with a wide variety of children's books can encourage their children to read specific books that relate to their needs and discuss what they have read. A girl wouldn't hesitate to read Gary Paulsen's *Hatchet* (1987), which features Brian Robeson, a male protagonist, but how many boys have had the pleasure of reading Jean George's *Julie of the Wolves* (1972) or Louise Fitzhugh's *Harriet the Spy* (1964)? Boys are expected to exhibit virility, especially during adolescence, and may feel that showing interest in a book with a girl in the title role, no matter how good that book might be, would not be considered "manly." On the other hand, it is considered acceptable in a male-oriented society for adolescent girls to read books featuring boys. But the problems a character like Harriet faces have nothing to do with gender, and Julie's struggles to survive on the Alaskan tundra reflect the same strength of character exhibited by Paulsen's Brian. Stories with strong female characters have to do with behavior, morality, and social conflicts, and apply to boys as well as girls.

OVERVIEW

What Are Little Girls Made Of? explores the ways in which selected children's books define female identity, especially when a female character is given a major role.

Chapter 1 discusses the relationship between text and artwork in picture books and the way in which girls can be made to feel rejected or empowered at a very early age, depending on the books read to them. The picture books presented conform to the subject matter of the chapters that follow: role models, historical eras, cultural backgrounds, social issues, social perceptions, controversial characters, and future innovations in children's books.

Chapter 2 highlights the qualities that cause certain female characters to gain the status of role models, setting standards that today's young women might do well to emulate.

Although some female characters in children's historical literature have been limited by the conventions of their times, others have emerged as heroes to their readership. Chapter 3 evaluates various female characters in the context of their specific historical periods.

Chapter 4 explores the cultural aspects of female identity in children's books that feature characters from a variety of racial and ethnic backgrounds.

Examined in Chapter 5 are children's books that address specific personal and social issues that affect a number of young women: homosexuality, physical or mental impairment, divorce, mental illness, obesity, various forms of addiction (such as eating disorders, alcoholism, or drug dependence), and any other area that might cause a girl to consider herself different from everyone else.

Chapter 6 looks at selected popular series fiction and other widely popular books that influence, for better or worse, the way young girls perceive themselves as they enter adolescence.

The topics of contrary and controversial female characters in children's books, and the debate about their influence on readers are found in Chapter 7.

Finally, looking ahead to the new millennium, Chapter 8 discusses current children's books and female authors and illustrators who present innovative formats and propose new roles for women. It also examines recent books that either continue to relegate female characters to a lesser role or ignore them altogether.

Each chapter is followed by an annotated bibliography, which includes a capsule review of each title. Not all titles in the bibliographies are discussed in the chapters, but they are listed to provide parents, teachers, and young people a broader base from which to choose when a particular subject is of special interest. In Chapter 1, the books in the bibliography are all picture books. Most picture books are read aloud to children by adults, in which case the reading level usually is not as important as the child's level of experience and familiarity with the subject matter. The remaining bibliographies are categorized by reading level, as follows:

EARLY READING   Ages 5–9. The child has basic reading skills and prefers simple vocabulary and story lines.

MIDDLE READING   Age 9–12. Reading skills have progressed to a point where the child prefers chapter books and more complicated vocabulary and story lines.

YOUNG ADULT   Ages 12 and up. Reading skills are taken for granted, and the reader wants to be challenged by story content.

At the end of the book is an appendix of recommended titles that explore particular personal qualities or values. This appendix includes several books not listed elsewhere in the body of this work; the decision to include them in the appendix was based primarily on published reviews. This appendix is followed by a research bibliography and index.

NOTES

1. Ida Harper Simpson. "The Modern Family," *Microsoft Encarta 96 Encyclopedia.* Copyright ©1995 Microsoft Corporation.
2. Marjorie N. Allen. *100 Years of Children's Books in America: Decade by Decade.* New York: Facts On File, 1996, p. 258.
3. Mary Pipher. *Reviving Ophelia: Saving the Selves of Adolescent Girls.* New

York: Ballantine Books, 1994, p. 18.

4. Patricia Aburdene and John Naisbitt. *Megatrends for Women: From Liberation to Leadership.* Rev. ed. New York: Fawcett Books, 1993, p. 350.

5. Lynn Sherr. *Failure Is Impossible.* New York: Times Books, 1995, p. xix.

6. Allen, p. 51.

7. Connie C. Epstein. "Publishing Children's Books." In *Children's Books and Their Creators: An Invitation to the Feast of Twentieth-Century Children's Literature,* edited by Anita Silvey. Boston: Houghton Mifflin, 1995, pp. 541–542.

8. The Newbery Medal is named for 18th-century English bookseller John Newbery.

9. The Caldecott Medal is named for 19th-century English illustrator Randolph Caldecott.

1

WORDS AND PICTURES: SEEKING SELF

Picture-book people are more easily condemned than almost any other artists in creation because we're dealing with such a volatile subject—children.

—Maurice Sendak,
Caldecott & Co.

A child's first experience with books usually occurs before the child knows how to read. Through picture books, children learn new things, reinforce what they have already learned, and connect books with life's experiences. When parents read to their children, they establish a foundation children can build on throughout their lives. It's important for adults to know what constitutes a good picture book so that they can choose wisely the books they read to children. The books should be judged on the quality of both text and pictures. Good picture books are interactive, drawing a child into the story and maintaining interest from one page to the next. The text must be complete in itself; the pictures become the illustrator's interpretation of the text. Together, the two art forms combine to add a new level of enjoyment. In the process of judging the worth of a picture book, the fact that the protagonist is a girl, a boy, or an animal matters less than it does in books for older readers, although many picture books do depict female characters in important roles.

ROLE MODELS

Maurice Sendak is best known for *Where the Wild Things Are* (1963), in which a small boy, Max, controls the "wild things" on his imaginary journey to a far-away island. This picture book has become the prototype for quality in the picture-book genre. The fact that the protagonist is a boy is irrelevant; there is absolutely nothing in this book that would discourage a girl from imagining herself in Max's place. But *Wild Things* is only one of a body of work by Sendak, who ignores political correctness in the interest of creativity. If a story demands a female protagonist, he creates one. A case in point is a book written before *Wild Things* called *The Sign on Rosie's Door* (1960), based on one of Sendak's childhood neighbors in Brooklyn. Rosie is a leader who uses her imagination and sense of purpose to create her own theater group on the streets of Brooklyn. She is very sure of who she is, literally and artistically.

When a picture book features a girl with overall appeal who stays true to her identity, it's a cause for celebration. Patricia Lee Gauch

Elise Primavera's lively illustrations in Christina Katerina and the Time She Quit the Family *(1987) by Patrica Lee Gauch portray the feisty young lady that Christina's fans have come to expect.*

created Christina Katerina in 1971 (*Christina Katerina and the Box*) and 16 years later wrote another book about her, *Christina Katerina and the Time She Quit the Family* (1987), maintaining Christina's resourceful nature and showing that this girl has strength of character and staying power. Two more books about her by Patricia Lee Gauch have followed: *Christina Katerina and the Great Bear Train* (1990) and *Christina Katerina and Fats and the Great Neighborhood War* (1997).

Joanna Cole's Magic School Bus series of books, illustrated by Bruce Degen, feature an independent, energetic, and somewhat eccentric science and math teacher named Ms. Frizzle. Ms. Frizzle's self-confidence and knowledge of her subject are refreshing, and her students love her. *The Magic School Bus on the Ocean Floor* (1992) offers subtle humor as Ms. Frizzle takes her students beneath the sea in the magic school bus. Degen's tongue-in-cheek cartoon-style drawings give Ms. Frizzle an appropriate wardrobe—with thermometers as earrings before the trip, life preserver earrings as they set out for the ocean, and a dress related to each subject that interests her.

Emily Arnold McCully, author and illustrator of *Mirette on the High Wire* (1992), is equally successful at creating a strong female character in her picture books. McCully was awarded the 1993 Caldecott Medal for *Mirette*, and the book definitely meets all the criteria for excellence in a picture book. The story about a young girl in Paris who has aspirations to become a famous high-wire walker combines in-depth characterizations with emotional tension, suspense, and a satisfying conclusion. McCully's sweeping, dramatic watercolor illustrations are a major departure from her picture books from the 1980s (*Picnic* and *School*), which, though delightful, were far more simplistic in execution. The artwork in *Mirette* captures the details of life in a Paris boardinghouse at the turn of the century, and each spread focuses directly on Mirette as she perseveres in her struggle to learn the skills of a wire walker.

HISTORICAL ERAS

Eve Bunting has usually tackled controversial themes in her picture books, but two of her most recent titles instead present in simple language widely diverse periods in history. Few fictional books for children focus on ancient Egypt, so the text of *I Am the Mummy Heb-Nefert* (1997) is exceptional in its ability to explain a great deal in a few well-chosen phrases. The book takes readers back to early Egyptian civilization through the words of a mummified Egyptian princess, who from a museum display case relates the history of her short life. The illustrations by David Christiana, in the style of Egyptian hieroglyphics, add a rich tapestry of color to the simple text.

Bunting explores the 19th-century American practice of sending urban orphan children west by train to be adopted by rural families along the route in *Train to Somewhere* (1996). The story is told from the viewpoint of a young girl, Marianne, who considers herself unappealing and has little hope of ever being chosen by a family. The pathos of the story is enhanced by the simple but moving illustrations by Ronald Himler.

The Revolutionary War comes alive in the Collier brothers' *My Brother Sam Is Dead* (1974), in which the protagonist is 12-year-old Tim, whose father and brother are fighting on opposite sides. His father is a Tory and his brother, Sam, is fighting for the Patriots, and Tim is divided in his loyalties. Tim's confusion increases when his father dies on a British prison ship and Sam, as an example to others, is executed by his own commanding officer for a crime he didn't commit.

The experience of women in that war is the focus of Patricia Lee Gauch's *This Time, Tempe Wick?* (1974), which celebrates a female Revolutionary War hero who never allows herself to be intimidated by the troops stationed on her property. Ann Turner's *Dakota Dugout* (1985) is a nostalgic and poetic account of a woman's experiences traveling west to settle in a house made of sod on the prairie. Illustrator Ronald Himler captures the isolation of such a life in spare, earth-tone illustrations.

CULTURAL BACKGROUNDS

Picture books also offer a visual introduction to different cultures, and Sook Nyul Choi, who was educated in the United States and taught school for several years, offers a Korean view of America in her first picture book, *Halmoni and the Picnic* (1993). Through the story of Yunmi, a Korean-American girl who has grown up in New York City, and her grandmother, Halmoni, a recent immigrant who avoids speaking English because she's ashamed of her accent, the book helps readers understand the barriers faced by the immigrant population.

Paul Goble, noted for his Native American picture books, illustrates the customs of the Plains Indians in words and pictures with *Beyond the Ridge* (1989), the story of an old woman who is dying. Death becomes a journey to peace and happiness as the woman joins her mother and other deceased relatives in an abundant natural world.

Mexican culture is well served by Tony Johnston's *Day of the Dead* (1997), with the brightly colored illustrations of Jeanette Winter making the festival of the dead a joyous occasion. Although the story does not focus exclusively on a female character, it depicts a brother and sister who are equally respected by the adults in a close-knit extended family. The details of preparations leading to this important holiday—gathering fruit and sugar cane, baking bread, making pastries, and bringing home marigolds from the market—build suspense as the children wait for this special day that honors the memory of their grandparents.

SOCIAL ISSUES

Addressing a way of life that some people consider deviant is difficult at the adult level; to do so at the picture-book level and to succeed in presenting well-adjusted people leading a normal life, as in Lesléa Newman's picture book *Heather Has Two Mommies* (1989), illustrated by Diana Souza, calls for a tribute to the book's creators. This book has created sufficient controversy to give it wide distribution, not because of how it is written, but because of what it's about. It deals with a child whose parents are a lesbian couple, and it is one of very few children's books to address lesbianism in any way. The story puts more emphasis on all the different family combinations possible in today's society than on details about Heather's

Mandy *by Barbara Booth, illustrated by Tim LaMarchen, presents the world of a deaf girl as she sees and experiences it.*

family life. There is no tension in the story, no exploration of the difficulties that might be faced by a child whose classmates could reflect a parent's prejudices, even in a school that celebrates diversity, as is the case here. Nevertheless, even a somewhat flawed presentation is better than no presentation at all. In *Mandy* (1991) by Barbara Booth, the main character is deaf and has been since birth. This enlightening picture book presents Mandy's world as she sees and experiences it. The things that frighten her are not the things she can see, but those she can't see. She hates the dark because it makes her feel so alone. But when her grandmother loses her favorite brooch, Mandy braves the dark with a flashlight to find it.

BIASED MESSAGES

The majority of picture books in publisher's catalogs feature boys or androgynous animals, and in bookstores the majority of picture books on display feature boys on the covers. This is perhaps a marketing decision. Author Mindy Bingham notes that "while girls are willing to read books about boys, it's been shown that the opposite is not true. Boys overwhelmingly reject any book or toy that is the least bit 'girlish.'"[1] Bingham goes on to say that "Contemporary picture books are often confusing. They may say that girls are smart or brave, but the underlying message may be quite different. The female 'hero' is still often rescued by a male, for example, or the illustrations show female characters standing idly by as the males work, act, or make decisions."[2]

Three recent and highly acclaimed picture books have no female characters, standing by or otherwise. *Animal Dreaming: An Aboriginal Dreamtime Story* (1998) by Paul Morin is an Australian Aborigine creation story, and the boy Mirri is told the story by the tribal elder Gadurra. The illustrations are spectacular, but the role of the female in the Australian Aboriginal people's mythology is virtually absent. *Amistad Rising: A Story of Freedom* (1998) by Veronica Chambers omits any female presence in this story of Joseph Cinque. Cinque is taken from his home to be a slave and, convinced he and the rest of the slaves will be killed before reaching America, rebels against the captain and crew and takes over the ship. Paul Lee's dramatic illustrations show no women on the ship or at the trial. Similarly, Ed Young, whose picture books have been highly acclaimed for many years, recently wrote and illustrated a story called *The Lost Horse: A Chinese Folktale* (1998) without including a single female character. The illustrations are beautifully rendered and true to a Chinese style of art. On the back cover a plastic sleeve contains cardboard puppet characters that children are encouraged to use in imaginative play. As a book for boys, it has merit, although the text doesn't measure up to the illustrations. For girls interested in Chinese folktales, *The Song of Mu Lan* and *Beautiful Warrior: The Legend of the Nun's Kung Fu* (see pages 29–30) focus directly on female Chinese heroes.

UNCONVENTIONAL CHARACTERS

Two unconventional females—one human, one animal—who have carved a place in literary picture-book history are the plucky star of Ludwig Bemelmans's *Madeline* (1939), and Martha, the irresistible prima donna of Susan Meddaugh's *Martha Speaks* (1992). In the first book, the difference between Madeline and her 11 schoolmates is not immediately evident—they're all dressed exactly alike—but partway through the book, Madeline begins to stand out:

> The smallest one was Madeline.
> She was not afraid of mice—
> she loved winter, snow, and ice.
> To the tiger in the zoo
> Madeline just said, "Pooh-pooh."

She manages to become very much an individual as she, the smallest of the 12, is measured for an outfit, greets a mouse, and stands up to a tiger. When Madeline has her appendix removed, all the other little girls at Miss Clavell's school want to be just like her.

Martha, on the other hand, is a family dog who shows her individuality at the outset, and when she eats some alphabet soup, she is suddenly able to talk. As the text tells Martha's story, voice balloons in the cartoon-like illustrations add dialogue between Martha and her family.

Although Roger Duvoisin's *Petunia* (1950) features a goose in the title role, she is a "liberated female, born in the Fifties with a vision of the Nineties."[3] Petunia believes in herself to a fault, and her self-confidence convinces her friends that whatever she tells them is right. They follow her advice and discover to their dismay that

Petunia is wrong. It is to Petunia's credit that she admits her mistakes and sets out to rectify them.

A character who might be considered the picture-book version of the controversial Harriet (see *Harriet the Spy,* pages 115–117) is Eloise, an independent six-year-old who lives at the Plaza Hotel in New York City with a nanny, a day maid, a night maid, and a tutor. Her parents don't have time for her, and she has no one to confide in. *Eloise* (1955) by Kay Thompson is a sophisticated portrait of a "precocious" child that appeals to both children and adults.

INNOVATIONS

Audrey and Don Wood are noted for innovative picture books, but *Bright and Early Thursday Evening: A Tangled Tale* (1996) is truly a book of the 1990s. They have put aside the typical picture book format that introduces in a specific setting a protagonist who is faced with a problem that at first defies solution but finally is resolved. Instead, Don Wood's complex illustrations, which are computer designed and generated, include, for example, a double spread of conflicting symbols—a colorful riot of flowers amid dark gravestones under an angry moon and a fully grown woman in a cradle decorated with skulls. Audrey's text accompanying the spread contradicts both itself and the illustration:

> Bright and early Thursday evening
> I woke up and dreamed I was dead.

With death at the beginning of this book and birth at the end, new beginnings are endlessly possible: "There's an end in every beginning. So if you believe a word that I've said, Begin again, please, at the ending."

In this electronic age, any event that makes it to television or film immediately establishes a market for books about the subject. Because Disney films are so widely advertised and are made interactive with tie-in products, books adapted by Disney benefit from the associated marketing effort. Jeanne M. Lee's *The Song of Mu Lan* (1995) was published before *Mulan,* the movie, debuted in June

1998. Fortunately, Lee's picture book has all the qualities that give it literary worth and make it a logical choice for children, parents, teachers, and librarians interested in a deeper involvement with Mu Lan's story. The text is a translated Chinese folk poem dated between the fifth and sixth century A.D., nicely edited by Lee, about the daughter of a man who is drafted into the emperor's army because he has no sons. The daughter, Mu Lan, takes her father's place by disguising herself as a boy. The book features carefully composed pencil illustrations, and includes the Chinese text in finely wrought calligraphy:

> A male rabbit is fast and agile,
> A female rabbit has bright eyes.
> When two rabbits run together,
> No one can tell which is male, which is female.

Another picture book highlighting female heroism is Emily Arnold McCully's *Beautiful Warrior: The Legend of the Nun's Kung Fu* (1998). Illustrated in traditional Chinese art panels, the book represents McCully's versatility as she tells the story of two women in 17th-century China who learn strength through the calmness of kung fu: One, a warrior nun named Wu Mei, teaches the other, a desperate young woman, kung fu to defeat a bully.

The Day Gogo Went to Vote: South Africa, April 1994 (1996) is a story that could not have been told until the mid-1990s. Elinor Batezat Sisulu describes the day South Africa held its first democratic elections through the emotional story of Thembi's great-grandmother, Gogo, a black South African who hasn't left her property since she was treated badly at the pension office many years earlier. Now, finally, she can vote, and accompanied by Thembi she goes to the polls. She must join a long line of waiting voters, but these are people who have never been allowed to vote before in their lives, and the occasion is one of celebration.

The 20th century is considered the golden age of children's books in America, and the 1990s is the decade of the picture book. Picture books in brilliant color used to be cost prohibitive, but with computer advancements in the publishing industry, almost anything is possible. Content also has expanded to include any and all subjects, and the picture-book market has grown considerably. Expensive, artistic picture books are as much in demand as collectors' items as they are for gifts. With so many options, it becomes more and more difficult to make choices. Adults who take the time to determine the worth of a picture book before choosing it can create a demand for quality in both text and pictures.

NOTES

1. Mindy Bingham and Sandy Stryker. *Things Will Be Different for My Daughter.* New York: Penguin, 1995, p. 201.
2. Ibid.
3. Marjorie N. Allen. *100 Years of Children's Books in America: Decade by Decade.* New York: Facts On File, 1996, p. 140.

ANNOTATED BIBLIOGRAPHY

Bemelmans, Ludwig. *Madeline.* New York: Simon & Schuster, 1939; New York: Picture Puffin, 1977.

> Designed in cartoon-like double spreads with minimal text, this book highlights the charm of Madeline, who emerges as an individual in a group of 12 little girls who all look alike. Sketches of familiar Paris landmarks create a travelogue, and the Catholic school setting was a first in children's books. Madeline has her appendix removed and is left with a satisfying scar that is the envy of her 11 classmates and only enhances her individuality.

Booth, Barbara D. *Mandy.* Illus. Jim LaMarche. New York: Lothrop, Lee, & Shepard, 1991.

> Mandy, who lives with her grandmother, was born deaf. Her way of looking at the world is different from that of a hearing child: She uses her other senses to understand the way things might sound. She enjoys looking at the family photo album, and she enjoys dancing with her grandmother. Sometimes, she can feel the sound of the radio with her feet. But Mandy doesn't like darkness. The world outside at night seems to end at the edge of her flashlight beam. Even so, when her grandmother loses the brooch Grandpa gave her and she and Mandy can't find it during the day, Mandy decides to brave the darkness and try to capture the sparkle of the brooch with her

flashlight. When she trips and drops the flashlight, it seems that she will never find her way out of the darkness and perhaps no one will be able to find her.

Bunting, Eve. *I Am the Mummy Heb-Nefert*. Illus. David Christiana. San Diego: Harcourt Brace, 1997.

The mummy Heb-Nefert, "black as night, stretched as tight as leather on a drum," was a young Egyptian woman who married the brother of the pharaoh and led a happy, though short, life on the banks of the Nile in ancient Egypt. When she dies at the height of her beauty, she is anointed with oils, wrapped in linens, and, with her cat Nebut, is placed in a tomb. Years later Heb-Nefert is put on display in a museum, where the people who observe her, as the spirit of Heb-Nefert notes, will themselves one day be dust and bones.

———. *Train to Somewhere*. Illus. Ronald Himler. New York: Clarion Books, 1996.

The practice of sending orphans across the United States by train so that they could become family helpers is a matter of historical record. Bunting personalizes the practice by telling the story of one child, Marianne, who is torn between her desire to be chosen and her hope that her mother will be at one of the station stops to claim her. Marianne knows she is not attractive, is too shy, and lacks special abilities. When the train has only one more stop to make, Marianne is desolate. She hasn't found her mother, and she has yet to be chosen. At the station, one couple waits, and Marianne somehow knows her hopes are about to be realized.

Choi, Sook Nyul. *Halmoni and the Picnic*. Illus. Karen M. Dugan. Boston: Houghton Mifflin, 1993.

Korean-American Yunmi attends St. Patrick's Elementary School in New York City. She is comfortable with her classmates and with the American way of life. But when her grandmother, Halmoni, comes from Korea to stay, Yunmi worries about how her grandmother will be viewed by her American classmates. What could be a difficult situation is defused by Mrs. Nolan, Yunmi's teacher, and Halmoni never has to know of her granddaughter's concerns.

Cole, Joanna. *The Magic School Bus: At the Waterworks*. Illus. Bruce Degen. New York: Scholastic, 1986.

This is the first book in the Magic School Bus series, and it is difficult to find in bookstores. However, it sets the scene for future Magic School Bus picture books and introduces the teacher, Ms. Frizzle, whose independence and cleverness encourage girls with a scientific bent.

———. *The Magic School Bus on the Ocean Floor.* Illus. Bruce Degen. New York: Scholastic, 1992.

> The children in Ms. Frizzle's science class go on a trip beneath the ocean in the magic school bus and become directly involved with creatures of the deep. Ms. Frizzle is always confident of her own capabilities and manages to guide her students through danger with aplomb.

Duvoisin, Roger. *Petunia.* New York: Knopf, 1950. Reprinted in Duvoisin's *Petunia the Silly Goose Stories.* New York: Knopf, 1987.

> Petunia is a goose who believes in herself. In fact, when she finds a book, she becomes convinced that just by owning it she knows how to solve all problems. But Petunia doesn't know how to read, and soon discovers that her self-confidence is not backed by knowledge. The advice she gives her friends causes much confusion, until Petunia starts to learn the alphabet so that she can right all of her wrongs.

Fox, Mem. *Whoever You Are.* Illus. Leslie Staub. San Diego: Harcourt Brace, 1997.

> Using a primitive type of folk art with bright colors and simple pictures, this picture book by Australian author Mem Fox celebrates both diversity and similarity in a format similar to Audrey Wood's *Birdsong* (see page 33). This book focuses on the children in different parts of the world who are as much a part of the natural world as any other animal.

Gauch, Patricia Lee. *Christina Katerina and the Box.* Illus. Doris Burn. New York: Coward, McCann, 1971.

> Christina Katerina is a resourceful and highly motivated girl. She transforms an empty refrigerator box into a backyard castle and thoroughly enjoys entertaining her stuffed bears in it. When her friend Fats Watson sneaks into her castle while she's at lunch, Christina Katerina locks him in and doesn't let him out until he hollers "I'm sorry" 15 times. Fats gets back at her by tipping over her castle, but Christina is unperturbed. She turns the box into a clubhouse. When Fats stages a sit-in on the roof and caves it in, the box becomes a race car. Christina Katerina keeps moving forward, never allowing adversity to discourage her, and it becomes obvious that nothing will ever stop this determined young woman.

———. *Christina Katerina and the Time She Quit the Family.* Illus. Elise Primavera. New York: Coward, McCann, 1987.

The strength of character exhibited by Christina Katerina has established her as an individual who knows her own mind. Even though a different artist portrays her in this story, 16 years after Gauch created her, she is still the same feisty young woman who does as she pleases, in this case discovering through her own actions what works for her and what doesn't. When Christina is blamed for something her brother has done, she announces she is quitting the family. She changes her name to Agnes, calls her mother Mildred, and divides the house into "hers" and "theirs." In her area, she is free to do what she wants, and for a while it's satisfying. But the novelty wears off, and Christina Katerina reassesses her priorities.

————. *This Time, Tempe Wick?* Illus. Margot Tomes. New York: Coward, McCann, 1974.

Gauch's story of Tempe Wick is an energetic retelling of an event that took place during the Revolutionary War. Tempe is taller than other girls and stronger than most men. She matches her father for endurance when the plowing has to be done and is able to beat him in a race on her horse Bonny. She maintains an even disposition and doesn't flaunt her abilities. But when George Washington's Pennsylvania troops, who are spending the harsh winter in Jockey Hollow, stage a mutiny and one of the soldiers demands Tempe's horse, she shows her true colors, exhibiting courage, ingenuity, and resourcefulness in the face of danger.

Goble, Paul. *Beyond the Ridge.* New York: Bradbury Press, 1989.

An elderly woman knows she is dying, and in the custom of the Plains Indians, she leaves her body to join her mother, who is calling her. Instead of considering death as an unknown end, Goble shows it from the viewpoint of the dying woman— as a pathway of great beauty leading to an abundant natural world where the woman joins her mother and other deceased relatives and experiences great peace. In a note at the beginning of this picture book, Goble tells of a Lakota woman who makes dolls without facial features because "children give the dolls their own personality, and do not have it dictated to them by the maker."

Johnston, Tony. *Day of the Dead.* Illus. Jeanette Winter. San Diego: Harcourt Brace, 1997.

The colorful illustrations in this small picture book build in suspense as sister and brother wait for the special autumn celebration that lies ahead in honor of the family's dead.

"*Espérense*—wait," the relatives tell them, as each member of this extended family gathers fruit and sugar cane, bakes bread, makes pastries, and brings home marigolds from the market. At night, they gather everything together and go with other families to the graveyard in remembrance of *los abuelos*—the grandparents. Everyone dances, sings, and eats, welcoming the spirits of their loved ones, who are thought to take part in this Mexican equivalent of All Souls' Day known as *el día de los muertos* (the Day of the Dead). Although the focus of this book is on family togetherness rather than female character development, its message, with a simple text and brightly colored pictures, clearly portrays the respect shown to Mexican children as well as unequivocal acceptance of them, no matter what the gender.

Lattimore, Deborah Nourse. *Frida Maria: A Story of the Old Southwest* and *Frida María: Un cuento del sudoeste de antes.* San Diego: Harcourt Brace, 1994.

A small girl who lives on a ranch in southern California when it was a Mexican territory makes ready for Fiesta, but while her mother wants her to be a proper señorita, Frida would much rather ride her horse, Diablo. Though she tries to please her mother at the fiesta, she can't resist helping her uncle when it appears his horse is losing a race with that of the mayor of a neighboring town. Frida jumps on Diablo and wins the race for her uncle. The double printing of this book, one version in English and one version in Spanish, and the details of Spanish influence in southern California have merit, but the storyline is rather slight.

Lee, Jeanne M. *The Song of Mu Lan.* New York: Front Street Books, 1995.

When Mu Lan's father is drafted into the army of the emperor because he has no sons, his daughter, Mu Lan, disguises herself as a boy and takes his place. She becomes a highly esteemed warrior, spending 12 years as a soldier, then returns home and surprises her fellow soldiers when she discards her soldier's gear and dresses as the woman she is.

McCully, Emily Arnold. *Beautiful Warrior: The Legend of the Nun's Kung Fu.* New York: Scholastic, 1998.

When a female child shows great intelligence, her father refuses to let her feet be bound, a practice that was intended to keep wealthy Chinese women at home and idle, and allows her to pursue an education. She studies martial arts and becomes a

Buddhist nun named Wu Mei. When she saves a young girl from a forced marriage, she teaches the girl the art of kung fu so that she can protect herself from the man's unwanted attentions. Balance, rather than force, leads the girl to success in her confrontation with the man who is trying to subdue her.

————. *Mirette on the High Wire.* New York: G.P. Putnam's Sons, 1992. CALDECOTT MEDAL.

Mirette lives in 19th-century Paris. Her mother runs a boarding house, and when she rents a room to the mysterious Bellini, Mirette discovers that he was once known as the Great Bellini, master wire walker. She begs him to teach her to walk across the tight wire; although he agrees, he himself will not walk the wire because, he tells her, he has become fearful. Mirette refuses to accept his lack of confidence. When he finally agrees to perform on the wire and then is unable to cross, she sets out across the wire to meet him. He has no choice; for the sake of his young protégée, he has to overcome his fear.

————. *Popcorn at the Palace.* San Diego: Harcourt Brace, 1997.

Maisie Ferris lives on a farm in Galesburg, Illinois, at the time of Queen Victoria's reign in England. Because she has expanded her knowledge of the world by reading magazines such as *Knickerbocker* and *Godey's* in addition to the family Bible, one of her dreams is to travel to Europe and meet the queen. A discerning Maisie informs a visiting journalist from England that one of the farm's fields happens to be of popcorn, which the journalist has never heard of, and when Maisie's father decides to take some cattle *and* the popping corn to England, Maisie speaks up. "I want to see the Queen. . . . It was my idea, Papa. And I could be a help to you." In England, Maisie, who is determined to make her dream come true, has an audience with Queen Victoria.

MacLachlan, Patricia. *Mama One, Mama Two.* Illus. Ruth Lercher Bornstein. New York: Harper, 1982.

Maudie finds it difficult to accept her mother's unhappiness and isolation from others, even from her own daughter. Her mother stays in her room; Maudie has to do all the cooking and cleaning, and sometimes she has nothing to eat but crackers. But when her mother has to go away to a place that will help her feel better, Maudie is devastated. She is sent to live with a foster mother named Katherine. As it turns out, Katherine understands completely how Maudie feels and helps her deal with her feelings through storytelling—about

Maudie's mother, who will be back in the spring, and about herself, Katherine, who will be there for Maudie until her mother comes home.

Meddaugh, Susan. *Martha Speaks*. Boston: Houghton Mifflin, 1992.
When Helen gives her alphabet soup to Martha, the family dog, the family has an unexpected surprise: "The letters in the soup went up to Martha's brain instead of down to her stomach," and "that evening, Martha spoke." Martha knows how to speak, but she doesn't know enough to stop. She becomes such a nuisance that the family stops giving her alphabet soup. One night, when the family is out, a thief breaks into the house, and when Martha dials 911, all she can do is bark. To keep her quiet, the thief gives her leftover alphabet soup from a pot on the stove. When the family returns, the police are at the house. "We got a call at the station," says a policeman. "Some lady named Martha." With expressive illustrations and commentary in voice balloons supplementing the low-key text, Meddaugh's Martha is an unlikely but very likeable hero.

Newman, Lesléa. *Heather Has Two Mommies*. Illus. Diana Souza. Northampton, Mass.: In Other Words Publishing, 1989.
Two women who love each other want to have a child, and, through artificial insemination, they do. The child is Heather, and the first part of the picture book deals with the steps followed to bring about Heather's birth and the nurturing she receives from her two mothers. The second part covers nursery school for Heather and introduces several children in various settings—Miriam, who has a mommy and a baby sister but no father; Stacy, who has two daddies; Joshua, who has a mommy, a daddy, and a stepdaddy; Juan, who has a mommy, a daddy, and a big brother; and David, who, like his brothers and sisters, is adopted. One of David's brothers is in a wheelchair. Heather, who has two mommies, is made to feel comfortable in this diverse environment.

Rathmann, Peggy. *Ruby the Copycat*. New York: Scholastic, 1991.
Ruby is the new girl at school and in order to fit in she follows Angela's lead, doing whatever Angela does. But Angela, who at first doesn't mind Ruby tagging along, discovers that Ruby is making claims that are true for Angela but not for Ruby. With the help of an understanding teacher, Ruby manages to implement her own way of seeing things and the friendship that ensues is because of who Ruby is, not who she can be like.

Schields, Gretchen. *The Water Shell*. San Diego: Harcourt Brace, 1995.

The female role is important in the mythology of the Polynesian islands—from the Fire Queen, who destroys a perfect world, to the child Keiki, who restores a world less perfect but capable of rejuvenation. Schields has incorporated into one story many of the mythological beliefs of these South Pacific islands, including Tahiti, Hawaii, the Marquesas, the Society Islands, Samoa, and Easter Island.

Sendak, Maurice. *Maurice Sendak's Really Rosie Starring the Nutshell Kids.* New York: Harper, 1975.

This is one of the earliest examples of a picture book leading to a television program. The original story of Rosie was published in 1960; it was called *The Sign on Rosie's Door* and featured a girl of driving force. The prototype for Rosie was Sendak's childhood neighbor in Brooklyn. The newer version, *Really Rosie,* was televised as a musical play, starring Rosie, who sings, acts, taps, and serves as director for her group of performers, the Nutshell Kids.

———. *Outside Over There.* New York: Harper, 1981.

Though Sendak's best-known picture books feature male characters, this follow-up to *Where the Wild Things Are* (1963) focuses on Ida, who resents having to take care of her baby sister and pays little attention to her. But when her sister is kidnapped by goblins, Ida bravely follows to rescue the baby. Like Max in *Where the Wild Things Are,* Ida tames the goblins and brings her sister home.

Sisulu, Elinor Batezat. *The Day Gogo Went to Vote: South Africa, April 1994.* Boston: Little, Brown, 1996.

Thembi and her great-grandmother, Gogo, are very close. They understand each other well. It is therefore surprising to Thembi when Gogo insists on going to the polls to vote. Gogo hasn't left her yard for many years after being treated badly at the pension office. But things have changed in South Africa: Apartheid has ended, and the people of the community are able to vote for the first time ever. Thembi accompanies her great-grandmother to the polls, and the people of the community, even the election official, welcome Gogo on this historic occasion.

Thompson, Kay. *Eloise.* Illus. Hilary Knight. New York: Simon & Schuster, 1955, 1969.

Eloise, a seemingly self-sufficient six-year-old, is the subject of this picture book depicting urban apartment living and less-than-ideal family life at a time in America's social history when children's books tended to focus on ideal families, small towns, and happy endings. Instead of warm, understanding parents and grandparents, Eloise lives in the Plaza hotel and has a nanny, a day maid, a night maid, and a tutor.

Turner, Ann. *Dakota Dugout.* Illus. Ronald Himler. New York: Macmillan, 1985.

This picture book reflects upon a time in history when pioneer women traveled by train across the country to join their husbands. They lived in homes made of sod, with the wind blowing through the walls in winter, and the corn dying up in the summer during long, discouraging droughts. Over time, the family in the story replaces their dugout with a clapboard house, with cushioned furniture and slippery floors, but the memories of the Dakota dugout grow sweeter with time.

Wood, Audrey. *Birdsong.* Illus. Robert Florczak. San Diego: Harcourt Brace, 1997.

The Woods, Audrey and Don, are noted for their humor and word play, as in *The Napping House* (1984) and *King Bidgood's in the Bathtub* (1985), two "predictable" picture books, very popular with young children. These books were coined "predictable" in the 1980s because they contained repetitive phrases that allowed a child listening to them to "predict" what the next line would be. But like many exceptionally talented people, this couple has used their popularity to branch into different areas of the picture-book genre. An example is Audrey Wood's poetic, essay-style text for this title. The story, which takes the reader from east to west, north to south, country to country, is based on her experience as a volunteer in wildlife rehabilitation. In each location the story focuses on the bird most apt to be found there and describes each bird's unique song. Florczak's double-spread page designs with patterned borders realistically portray each bird mentioned within its particular habitat. The children in the illustrations, usually a boy and a girl, are also indigenous to the background but secondary to the overall scenes.

Wood, Audrey, and Don Wood. *Bright and Early Thursday Evening: A Tangled Tale.* San Diego: Harcourt Brace, 1996.

This picture book might interest young children on a simple level, but older children and adults will appreciate its nuances of language and art. In this age of computers, it makes sense to create a picture book dependent entirely on electronic art, which Don Wood has done here, and Audrey has taken word play to an unusual level with an offbeat, rhyming text that begins with a funeral and ends with a birth. Like some modern art, it either will be labeled as brilliant or dismissed as bizarre.

2

DOWN THE RABBIT HOLE: CONFIRMING SELF

He took me for his housemaid . . . How surprised he'll be when he finds out who I am!

—Alice, in *Alice's Adventures in Wonderland* by Lewis Carroll

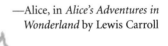

Classic heroes appear more often in fantasy than in realistic fiction. This is especially true in English fantasy, which draws from a wealth of material accumulated over the last thousand years through European fairy tales, folktales, and myth. Fantasy is a way for authors to explore basic truths as poets do. Their work becomes an analogy for real life, and each reader is likely to discover a different personal meaning. The fantasy genre, because it allows for different meanings, gives authors the freedom to explore social concerns more creatively than in realistic fiction. Such is the case with *Alice's Adventures in Wonderland* (1865) by English author Lewis Carroll.

As Alice travels through Wonderland, meeting obstacles and overcoming them, she becomes the female definition of a hero—not a heroine. In literature, a heroine tends to be the leading female character in a book, and she usually needs rescuing; a classic hero is self-sufficient and quite apt to rescue others. Heroes are never victims; they won't allow it. In contemporary society, as well as in children's literature, the role of victim is all too often applied to females; in the books discussed in this chapter, however, female protagonists solve their own problems.

REDEFINING HEROISM

Although Lewis Carroll knew that women and girls were capable of heroic feats, and so presented Alice, as recently as 1987 a hero was defined as "any *man* [my italics] noted for feats of courage or nobility of purpose."[1] In 1989, thanks to editor Judith Levey, the *Macmillan Dictionary for Children* presented the following definition of hero: "A person who is looked up to by others because of *his or her* [my italics] great achievements or fine qualities."[2]

In *Alice's Adventures in Wonderland*, Carroll's female protagonist fits the profile of the classic hero. Alice never gives rescue a thought. Like the literary heroes of old, she establishes a goal and is determined to fulfill it, even if it means her demise. When Alice decides to drink from the bottle labeled "drink me"—after checking to make sure it isn't marked "poison"—so that she can continue her journey, she starts to shrink rapidly and becomes concerned. "'It might end, you know,' said Alice to herself, 'in my going out altogether, like a candle.'" Nevertheless, when another occasion arises that calls for her to ingest an unknown substance in order to become her normal size, she doesn't hesitate to try it even though it too might cause her to "go out like a candle."

Alice doesn't see herself as a hero. She simply absorbs her adventures and notes at one point that she very well might be in the middle of a fairy tale. Through it all, she sustains her role as the main character and feels that there should be a book written about her. "And when I grow up, I'll write one," she says.

A strong sense of identity can be difficult for a female to attain in a world that has long relegated women to a lesser role. Even Alice, as she moves through Wonderland, begins to wonder who she really is because things are so strange; she starts thinking about children she knows who are her age and wonders if she could have been changed for any of them. The children she thinks about happen to be female—Ada and Mabel. She decides she isn't Ada, who wears her hair in ringlets. Since entering Wonderland, however, Alice seems to have forgotten all the things she used to know—multiplication tables and recitations—so she thinks that perhaps she is Mabel, "who knows so very little."

A BALANCED IDENTITY

The book's author, the Reverend Charles Dodgson, was an introvert who chose to write *Alice's Adventures in Wonderland* under the pseudonym Lewis Carroll. The story was written for eight-year-old Alice Liddell, a family acquaintance. Dodgson started telling the story to the Liddell children, making Alice the main character, beginning in 1862 when Dodgson and his friend Robinson Duckworth took the Liddell children on a river boating trip. He continued the stories through two more boating trips, but it wasn't until several months

The fairy tale could be defined as a story in which the characters, by means of a series of transformations, discover their true selves.

—Neil Philip, *The Complete Fairy Tales of Charles Perrault* later that he began writing them down and finally submitted the manuscript to a publisher.[3]

Carroll has given Alice none of the stereotypical traits generally attributed to females, such as weakness, unquestioning patience, timidity, and subservience. She displays a wide spectrum of qualities that go beyond gender. Alice is confident, responsible, caring, sensitive, and sensible, and has the ability to solve problems.

With the exception of *Alice's Adventures in Wonderland,* well-established English fantasy novels either avoid female protagonists almost entirely, as in J. R. R. Tolkien's *The Hobbit* (1937), or present nonspecific groups of children, male and female, as in C. S. Lewis's Chronicles of Narnia series (1950–1956). Richard Adams carried on the male-hero tradition in *Watership Down* (1972), in which the only females that appear require rescuing. Even though all of the characters are rabbits, they are portrayed with human traits, and only male heroes are featured.

Until the latter part of the 20th century, very few American authors excelled in the fantasy field. The majority of the best-known children's books in the fantasy genre have been written by authors from Europe and the British isles, where folk and fairy tales, told to an adult audience, formed the basis of fantasy in books for children.

American authors have given fantasy a new slant by combining magic and the forthright American viewpoint. One early American author who equated fantasy with his interpretation of the American dream[4] is L. Frank Baum, who introduced the indomitable Dorothy in *The Wonderful Wizard of Oz* (1900).

This illustration of Jinjur by John R. Neill appeared in the 1904 edition of L. Frank Baum's The Marvelous Land of Oz*.*

Although librarians did not consider Baum's writing to be of literary value,[5] Baum wrote a long series of popular Oz books. The second book, *The Marvelous Land of Oz* (1904), features a male protagonist, Tip, "small and rather delicate in appearance," who isn't quite what he seems. In fact, at the end of the story, it's revealed that Tip was born a girl, Princess Ozma, and has been under a spell. Tip resists having the spell lifted. When Glinda the Good Witch tells him he must resume his proper form and be Queen of the Emerald City, Tip says, "Oh, let Jinjur be the Queen. . . . I don't want to be a girl!" Nevertheless, the spell is lifted by Mombi the Sorcerer, and Princess Ozma takes her proper form, saying:

> "I hope none of you will care less for me than you did before. I'm just the same Tip, you know; only—only—"
> "Only you're different!" said the Pumpkinhead; and everyone thought it was the wisest speech he had ever made.

The same but different. A wise remark indeed.

Baum's mother-in-law was involved in the feminist movement, and it's quite possible that the section of the book dealing with General Jinjur's actions was an affectionate parody of his mother-in-law's efforts. Jinjur, who has taken over the Emerald City with her army of women, is captured and the throne is restored to Princess Ozma: "At once the men of Emerald City cast off their aprons. And it is said that the women were so tired of eating of their husbands' cooking that they all hailed the conquest of Jinjur with joy."

But it is Dorothy, more than Jinjur or Ozma, who can be considered a role model for today's young women. Like Alice, Dorothy finds herself in a strange new world, but instead of falling down a rabbit hole, she spins around inside a tornado and ends up in the land of Oz. Dorothy stoically accepts her strange fate and sets out on a journey to find her way back home. She meets dangers head on, and when her little dog Toto is threatened by a large lion, she rushes forward and slaps the lion as hard as she can on his nose. "Don't you dare bite Toto," she says. "You should be ashamed of yourself." The kind-hearted Dorothy befriends a scarecrow, a tin woodman, and even the lion, and they all join her on the yellow brick road that leads to the Kingdom of Oz and the great Wizard, who, it is hoped, will grant their wishes. But as it turns out, Dorothy gets her heart's desire—to go home—by her own efforts.

Alice and Dorothy seldom doubt their own capabilities. Aerin, on the other hand, in the opening pages of American author Robin McKinley's *The Hero and the Crown* (1984) is a king's daughter who has learned to "keep her mouth shut and smile on cue," a young woman who can be easily diminished by others and made to feel "smaller and shabbier than usual." This doesn't mean that Aerin accepts the role of submissive female. She can ride a horse with more skill than most men and wields a sword with aplomb. But she is not encouraged to pursue her aspirations. As her personal caretaker Teka comments: "You can't have believed your father would let you ride in the army. Few women do. . . ." But Aerin, as much as she tries to suppress her wish to be involved in the concerns of the kingdom, eventually realizes her fate is pre-ordained, and she goes resolutely into danger to fulfill her destiny. Only a great hero can slay the Black Dragon, Maur, last of the Great Ones, and Aerin finds herself on a quest to save her kingdom from the spell of evil by slaying Maur and regaining the Hero's Crown.

While Aerin's story focuses mainly on her personal development as a hero, Edith Pattou's *Hero's Song* (1991) features a male protagonist, Collun, who succeeds in his quest to destroy the White Dragon with the assistance of Brie, a female warrior. In this story, Collun considers himself cowardly and is more interested in gardening than battling a foe. When his sister, Nessa, is kidnapped by the evil Queen Mebd, Collun finally accepts his fate and sets out with his good friend Talisen, a bard, to find her. During his travels, he meets Brie, who is disguised as a boy. On more than one occasion, including the final battle, Brie saves Collun from certain death. Even Collun's sister, rather than waiting helplessly for rescue, takes her life into her own hands in an effort to escape from the dragon that holds her captive.

THE REAL WORLDS OF FANTASY

Fantasies often have more to do with reality than any so-called realistic fiction. Like poetry, fantasy touches on universal truths. It can become an allegory for social ills, a lesson in morality, a metaphor for proper values. The ancient myths, folktales, and fairy tales all had moral implications. In fact, one of the best-known storytellers in literary history, Charles Perrault, included a moral poem at the end of each story.

In *The Complete Fairy Tales of Charles Perrault* (1993), newly translated by Neil Philip and Nicoletta Simborowski, the familiar fairy tales, which had been softened over the years to protect children from the violence contained in the originals, are presented in their original form that Perrault once intended for an adult audience. In this version, Sleeping Beauty's story doesn't end when she is awakened by the prince. She marries him in secret and has two children—a boy and a girl. She and the prince do not live happily ever after as king and queen, at least not for quite some time, because the queen mother happens to be part ogre, and when she discovers she has a daughter-in-law and two grandchildren, she orders her son's family served up for dinner. It is, however, the queen mother who pays the price by diving into a vat and being "devoured in an instant by the foul creatures within," and "the king couldn't help grieving, for she was his mother, after all, but he soon consoled himself with his lovely wife and children."

Perrault, in recording these oral tales, included a sometimes macabre sense of humor. In "Little Red Riding Hood," the wolf first eats the grandmother, then Red Riding Hood, and no one comes to the rescue, the moral being "Don't talk to strangers," and don't climb into bed with your grandmother because "not every wolf runs on four legs." The moral of "Bluebeard" is that curiosity is a risky game, but a second moral is as follows, in part:

> Anyone with half an eye
> Can see this tale's of times gone by.
> No husband wants his wife to cower,
> Or thinks that she is in his power.

In "Cinderella," her stepsisters call her Cinderbutt, but there is more to this young woman than meets the eye. When she loses her slipper at the ball, and the prince searches for the owner, Cinderella speaks up and says to the prince, "Let me see if it fits me." She doesn't wait for good fortune to find her; she takes advantage of the moment.

The stories in these translations reflect a direct and simple style of writing, and there is a discussion at the end of the book of each story's origins and different interpretations over time. The basic premise of most retellings of these stories over the years is that the prince saves and then marries the beautiful damsel in distress and they live happily ever after. This collection not only contradicts that adage by portraying females with minds of their own but also restores the stories to include the tongue-in-cheek humor that made Perrault a great storyteller. These versions require a certain amount of experience on the part of the reader to be properly understood and, for young adults especially, could generate a lively discussion of fairy tales in general.

BRIDGE TO UNDERSTANDING

Fantasy offers a safe bridge to understanding between adults and children. Ann Turner makes the conflict between nature and the human condition the main theme of her fantasy *Elfsong* (1995), the first book in her Elfsong trilogy. Maddy, the book's main character, meets an elfin creature and must reassess her beliefs about what is possible and what is not.

Two American women whose fantasy writing for young people has achieved universal recognition and critical acclaim are Ursula K. Le Guin and Madeleine L'Engle. L'Engle expanded the definition of fantasy with *A Wrinkle in Time* (1962) and followed up with two more books in her Time Fantasy series, *A Wind in the Door* (1973) and *A Swiftly Tilting Planet* (1978). By featuring a female protagonist, Meg Murry, L'Engle veered from the expected "male hero experiencing his rite of passage" role, and gave young readers a role model in Meg that defied gender. L'Engle's books are revered by both boys and girls.

Although Le Guin's *A Wizard of Earthsea* (1968) introduces a male protagonist, the second book in the Earthsea series, *The Tombs of Atuan* (1971) features a female protagonist, Tenar, who ultimately comes full circle and realizes her potential and purpose in the fourth Earthsea novel, *Tehanu: The Last Book of Earthsea* (1990). The third book, *The Farthest Shore* (1971), is the least satisfying book in the series, perhaps because after creating a believable premise in the first two books with the intrigue between Tenar and the apprentice wizard Ged, the third doesn't meet the expectations of the reader. It is in the last book, *Tehanu*, that closure finally occurs.

FAIRY TALES AND MYTHS REVISITED

In classic fairy tales, girl meets boy and they live happily ever after, but such a future is not for everyone; in fact, happiness is a fleeting state that people experience off and on, rarely "ever after." Emma Donoghue's *Kissing the Witch: Old Tales in New Skins* (1997) is a tapestry of storytelling that features familiar fairy tales made over into new patterns. Cinderella discovers that her fairy god-mother has far more character than the rather shallow prince; Beauty's beast is a woman in disguise; Gretel saves her brother, Hansel, and stays behind with the witch. This is a collection of stories about identity and the power available to women who believe in themselves.

> If you see the magic in a fairy tale, you can face the future.
>
> —Danielle Steele

Virginia Hamilton has been awarded many prizes for her work, so it is ironic that her book *In the Beginning: Creation Stories from Around the World* (1988) overwhelmingly credits men as creators; women, when mentioned, are given a minor role, either giving birth to the creator or marrying him. Hamilton does make it clear that her stories are based on male interpretations of the myths. In the book *Her Stories: African American Folktales, Fairy Tales, and True Tales* (1995), as the title implies, Hamilton focuses on African-American stories "of the female kind" in an effort to give women their proper place in the history of storytelling. Unfortunately, although the stories and narratives in Hamilton's collection feature women, most of the versions she chooses do not give women assertive roles. These stories, says Hamilton, are from the plantation era, at which time the black slave woman was keeper of households, a laborer without pay—in contrast to the matriarchal order that existed in many parts of Africa, in which the mother was the sole guardian of the children, the property holder, and retainer of the family name.

In "Lena and Big One Tiger," Big One Tiger-Man marries Lena to let her know that "a woman can't be more than a man." The original story, Hamilton notes, might have been told by a male member of an African tribe as a protest against the matriarchal order. In "Little Girl and Buh Rabby," the little girl is an observer, following her mother's advice to keep the rabbit in the garden until "Daddy comes home." The rabbit is the clever one, and Daddy is the hero who dispatches Wolf. All of the stories presented by Hamilton in this book have a common thread regarding social attitudes toward women in African-American society. With few exceptions, they appear to be stories written about women by men reacting to the threat of their female counterparts, as in "Woman and Man Started Even." One of the few stories credited to a female storyteller is a tall tale about Annie Christmas, who, like John Henry, is larger than life, but even in this story, the indomitable Annie meets her downfall when she is rejected by a man. "Malindy and Little Devil," however, presents a resourceful young woman who not only gets what she wants but never has to compromise for it. She doesn't need the help of a man, and she's as clever as any rabbit. It's the only story in the book that doesn't take away or keep from a woman her ability to solve her own problems.

The illustrations in *Her Stories* belie the portraits of helpless females in a man's world described in most of the stories. Malindy and Annie Christmas are visual portrayals of female African-American pride.

In a society that clearly discriminates against those who do not fit the Anglo-Saxon mold—white, healthy, wealthy, and wise—*The Shadow Warrior* (1990) by Pat Zettner pairs Llyndreth, a fair and blue-eyed girl of the Solgant race, with Zorn, a small and dark goblin of the Danturin race, who calls himself Shadow Warrior. The two are brought together unexpectedly when Zorn is injured and Llyndreth, who is looking for her brother, finds it impossible to leave him to his fate. He then finds he cannot ignore the debt he owes her, and the two, with an unlikely guardian, Angborn the Giant, head for a safe haven. During their journey, a friendship forms between the three unlikely companions, and because of it, new understandings about identity occur. All three main characters find their negative beliefs about people from other races weakened by their growing friendship, which allows them to appreciate their similarities and accept their differences. The book negates those stereotypes that label groups of people as the enemy instead of making an effort to know and accept a person for who he or she actually is.

Patrice Kindl is a new voice in young adult literature, and she offers a refreshing and highly unusual blend of fact and fantasy in *Owl in Love* (1993), the story of a young woman questioning her role in life. Owl, at age 14, is having trouble enough dealing with her emotions, but she also happens to be a shape changer who spends a part of each day as an owl. Because of her unusual lifestyle and appetites, she finds it difficult to relate to her peers. Her owl identity clearly has dominated her earlier years, but as she matures, she finds her human side vying for control.

Fantasy literature is open to interpretation in a way that realistic fiction is not. In realistic fiction, the reader relates to characters, settings, and dilemmas that he or she might face in everyday life, but in fantasy, suspension of disbelief allows the reader to enter new worlds in which the ordinary rules do not apply. Fantasy still requires boundaries, but within those boundaries anything can happen. In *Alice's Adventures in Wonderland,* for example, Alice takes her adventure for granted and never doubts her ability to solve all dilemmas. Owl in *Owl in Love* knows how different she is from other young women her age, but she makes no effort to conform and learns to deal with her differences.

NOTES

1. Editors of Reader's Digest. *Reader's Digest Illustrated Encyclopedic Dictionary.* Pleasantville, N.Y.: Reader's Digest, 1987, p. 790.
2. Judith Levey, ed. *Macmillan Dictionary for Children.* New York: Simon & Schuster Children's, 1989, p. 349.
3. Cameron Newham. "The Alice Years July 1862–June 1868." Lewis Carroll Home Page. Available on-line. URL: http://www.lewiscarroll.org/cal/to1868.html. Updated on July 31, 1998.
4. Marjorie Allen. *100 Years of Children's Books in America: Decade by Decade.* New York: Facts On File, 1996, pp. 25–26.
5. Ibid, p. 28.

ANNOTATED BIBLIOGRAPHY

Baum, L. Frank. *The Wonderful Wizard of Oz.* Illus. W. W. Denslow. Chicago: George M. Hill, 1900; New York: New American Library, 1984. (Middle Reading)

When Dorothy and her dog, Toto, find themselves in a strange and colorful new world after being swept away by a tornado, Dorothy sets out resolutely to find a way back home. On the way, she picks up strays—a scarecrow, a tin woodman, and a cowardly lion—and becomes their leader, ultimately guiding them and herself toward each of their heart's desires and meeting danger head on.

————. *The Marvelous Land of Oz*. Illus. John R. Neill. Chicago: Reilly & Britton, 1904; New York: Dover, 1969. (Middle Reading)

Many authors would have capitalized on *The Wonderful Wizard of Oz* by simply retelling Dorothy's story, but Baum respected his young audience. Although he made the Scarecrow and Tin Woodman part of his second book, he created an additional cast of imaginative characters: Princess Ozma, under a spell as the boy Tip; Jack Pumpkinhead, the Sawhorse; and Mr. H. M. Wogglebug, T. E. (Highly Magnified and Thoroughly Educated). Baum's mother-in-law was an advocate of women's rights, and this was reflected in *The Marvelous Land of Oz* with General Jinjur and her army of women soldiers capturing Oz by using knitting needles as weapons and turning over the cleaning and baby-sitting chores to the men.

Carroll, Lewis [Charles Dodgson]. *Alice's Adventures in Wonderland*. Illus. John Tenniel. London: Macmillan, 1865; New York: Random House, 1946. (Young Adult)

Alice finds herself in a strange world when she follows the White Rabbit down the rabbit hole. No matter what threatens her, she manages to overcome it and go on with her travels through Wonderland. She is determined to follow this adventure to its logical conclusion, and just when she thinks the end has come, she finds herself home again, with the whole adventure nothing but a dream.

Donoghue, Emma. *Kissing the Witch: Old Tales in New Skins*. New York: HarperCollins, Joanna Cotler Books, 1997. (Young Adult)

Though this collection of stories is written in the style of old-time fairy tales, Prince Charming and "happily ever after" are not the final objective. These are stories about women and the way in which they search for and finally attain their goals of independence and pride in self. In "The Tale of the Bird," an abusive husband replaces a young woman's abusive family, and under his smothering protection, her freedom is lost. The woman rescues and nurses an injured swallow, and on the day she sets it free, she feels a flicker of independence and dares to hope she too can fly away. In "The Tale of the Apple," a young woman accepts an apple from a stepmother who is nothing like a mother figure and finds it is not poisoned at all but exactly what she needed; she leaves the dwarfs to return to the castle and her stepmother. Finally, in "The Tale of the Kiss," a woman who is past childbearing age allows the villagers to see her as a witch, which gives her the power to manipulate them. But when she is confronted by absolute innocence and unconditional love in the person of a young girl, she must decide if she is able to accept and give love.

Hamilton, Virginia. *Her Stories: African American Folktales, Fairy Tales, and True Tales.* Illus. Leo Dillon and Diane Dillon. New York: Blue Sky Press, 1995. (Middle Reading)

> This story collection, divided into five sections—animal tales, fairy tales, supernatural stories, folktales and legends, and true tales—offers four stories per section, and three true stories at the end. All feature women, but only "Malindy and Little Devil" and the true tales, narratives recorded in the 1920s and 1930s, present women as heroes; in fact, the true tales are told by women whose very survival in a society that considered them chattel made them heroic.

Kindl, Patrice. *Owl in Love.* Boston: Houghton Mifflin, 1993. (Young Adult)

> Owl is a 14-year-old who happens to be a shape changer. She is able to become an owl at will, and even in her human form, she has the coloring of an owl, with grayish skin and large eyes. Whether bird or human, her food source is live animals, and her physical appearance sets her apart from her peers. Owl has discovered her true love—her science teacher, Mr. Lindstrom—and she spends her nights in owl form observing him from a tree outside his bedroom window. The fact that he is 40 years old and has a wife and child doesn't bother her, but what does is how her dreams of happiness with Mr. Lindstrom keep clashing with the reality of her life. Owl finds herself in a quandary as she becomes embroiled in human relationships and unfamiliar feelings of compassion and empathy, and is forced to deal with her human side.

Le Guin, Ursula K. *A Wizard of Earthsea.* Berkeley: Parnassus, 1968; New York: Macmillan, 1992. *The Tombs of Atuan.* New York: Atheneum, 1971; New York: Macmillan, 1992. *The Farthest Shore.* New York: Atheneum, 1972; New York: Macmillan, 1992. *Tehanu: The Last Book of Earthsea.* New York: Atheneum, 1990. (Young Adult)

> The first book in Le Guin's Earthsea cycle, *A Wizard of Earthsea*, is about a young boy's search for identity and his realization

that abuse of power brings forth darkness. When the boy, an apprentice wizard named Sparrowhawk, unleashes his power without thought of consequence, he finds himself launched on a longtime quest to regain balance in his universe, the world of Earthsea. In *The Tombs of Atuan* the story continues with Arha, whose true name is Tenar, as she attempts to gain her freedom from her role as the guardian of the Tombs. Her life becomes intertwined with Sparrowhawk, now named Ged, and she is faced with a decision to choose either the freedom of light or the obligations of her life of darkness. *The Farthest Shore* follows Ged who searches for the source of darkness with his companions—Dragonlord, Archmage, and Arren, a young prince—when magic in Earthsea shows signs of ending in an evil bid for immortality. Tenar and Ged's story continues in *Tehanu* when Tenar cares for the dying Archmage; takes in Ged, who has lost his powers; and helps the disfigured and abused child Tehanu to fulfill her special destiny.

L'Engle, Madeleine. *A Wrinkle in Time.* New York: Farrar, Straus & Giroux, 1962; New York: Dell, 1976. NEWBERY MEDAL. (Middle Reading)

Meg Murry feels she doesn't really belong in her family. Everyone else in the family has a special talent, and she feels ordinary, especially with her lack of mathematical ability. Her mother and father are scientists, her youngest brother is a genius, and her twin brothers fit very well into any social scene. But when Meg finds herself "tesseracting" into the fifth dimension and discovers that it is up to her to save her father's life, she begins to understand and accept her own special identity.

McKinley, Robin. *The Hero and the Crown.* New York: Greenwillow, 1984. NEWBERY MEDAL. (Middle Reading)

Aerin, daughter of the king of Damar, overcomes the biased view of those in power against her involvement in the affairs of the kingdom. When Aerin realizes only she can save her people from annihilation by the forces of evil, she willingly sets out to confront the Black Dragon, Maur, and regain the Hero's Crown.

Pattou, Edith. *Hero's Song.* San Diego: Harcourt Brace, 1991. (Young Adult)

In this fantasy, based in part on Irish mythology, Collun is a young man who must search for his kidnapped sister, Nessa, but who would much prefer to stay at home and care for his garden. With his favorite gardening tool, made into a knife by his blacksmith father, Collun leaves home and in his travels gains an entourage consisting of his best friend, Talisan, a bard;

the ellyl Silien, an elflike creature from a race long distrustful of humans; a wizard, Crann; and Brie, a female archer. As they face great danger in their quest to find Collun's sister and to destroy the evil that threatens their world, it is Brie who more than once saves Collun's life, and it is Brie who helps Collun destroy the evil dragon and save his sister.

Philip, Neil, and Nicoletta Simborowski, trans. *The Complete Fairy Tales of Charles Perrault.* Illus. Sally Holmes. New York: Clarion, 1993. (Middle Reading)

In this collection of 11 well-known fairy tales that have been adapted over the years and issued in many different formats and interpretations, the stories have been translated directly from the original French. Based on oral storytelling at an adult level, Perrault wrote the stories as moral allegories. In this new translation, a sense of humor and moral verses add a light touch to stories that have a tendency to be starkly graphic and violent. Both Red Riding Hood and her grandmother are gobbled up, Bluebeard is a wife abuser and serial killer, and Cinderella makes sure she gets her man.

Turner, Ann. *Elfsong.* San Diego: Harcourt, Brace, 1995. (Early Reading)

Fantasy for younger readers has had a tendency to incorporate humor with magic, but Ann Turner in *Elfsong,* the first book in her Elfsong trilogy, focuses on the conflict between humans and the natural world when Maddy meets an elf in a magical forest and discovers she can talk to the elf and all the animals in the forest. Nata, the elf, who only wanted to see a human, becomes friendly with Maddy and her grandfather; this, in turn, threatens his relationship with the other elves. In the meantime, the forest is a sinister place where the Great Horned Owl seeks to destroy the elves, and Nata, banished from the clan because of his interaction with humans, must slay the creature.

Zettner, Pat. *The Shadow Warrior.* New York: Atheneum, 1990. (Young Adult)

Llyndreth is a girl who doesn't believe in magic and considers goblins the enemy. But when she embarks on a journey to find her brother, she ends up traveling with a giant, Angborn, who practices magic, and nursing a goblin, Zorn, back to health after she finds him injured and helpless. Llyndreth, who is fair skinned, is a member of the Solgant race; Zorn is dark skinned and a member of the Danturin race; Angborn is the last of his race, the Eodans. These three races are given the opportunity, through the efforts of the three young people, to join in peace and reunite their world.

3

WHEN GRANDMA WAS A FLAPPER: EXPLORING SELF

Nothing changes more constantly than the past; for the past that influences our lives does not consist of what actually happened, but of what men believe happened.

—Gerald White Johnson,
American Heroes and Hero Worship

In the 1930s, 1940s, and 1950s, studying history meant memorizing dates and facts from textbooks—Christopher Columbus discovered America in 1492, the Revolutionary War was fought from 1776–1781, Eli Whitney invented the cotton gin, and a stock market crash in 1929 brought about the Great Depression. Facts were learned by rote, and personalities were ignored. Who was Christopher Columbus? What happened when he landed in the New World? What did the natives think of his visit and how were they affected? Jane Yolen's *Encounter* (1992) answers these questions in a thought-provoking picture book written from the viewpoint of a young Taino boy who recognizes the threat to his people when Columbus lands on his shores. A great many books have been written for children about Christopher Columbus, but there are few about the Taino Indians and none at all about the females of Columbus's time. History textbooks in schools traditionally have ignored the role of women in the history of the world, and the subjects of personal profiles in history books tend to be men. Over the past few decades, however, children's books have recognized the role of women in history by dramatizing their daring exploits with good storytelling.

MEDIEVAL TIMES

"Shakespeare," E. L. Konigsburg writes in her young adult novel *A Proud Taste of Scarlet and Miniver* (1973), "was far better at writing of heroes than of heroines." Konigsburg's novel, based on 12th-century history, offers a lively portrait of Eleanor of Aquitaine, who, first as queen of France, then as queen of England, encouraged color and pageantry at court, much to the chagrin of her husbands, Louis VII and Henry II. Konigsburg manages to include a great deal of history in this novel, such as the volatile relationship between Henry II and Sir Thomas Becket, an explanation of the Plantagenet name, and why a certain section of Paris is called the Latin Quarter.

Karen Cushman also goes back to medieval times in *Catherine, Called Birdy* (1994) and *The Midwife's Apprentice* (1995), but her settings are less colorful than Konigsburg's, focusing as they do on peasants and poverty. Medieval superstition created wild explanations

In Karen Cushman's The Midwife's Apprentice *(1995), a young woman in medieval times finds her calling in midwifery.*

for the unknown, and women were apt to be persecuted as witches, although belief in magical powers made certain women popular as midwives. These same women also were blamed if a birth didn't go right.

Into this ignorant society is born Beetle, who is abandoned and left to her own devices in *The Midwife's Apprentice*. Midwife Jane Sharp discovers Beetle trying to keep warm in a dung heap and takes the child in as a servant. Over time, Beetle begins to accept herself as a person worthy of notice, especially as she learns from Jane the basics of midwifery and discovers that the villagers are beginning to respect her. She abandons the unsavory name of Beetle and calls herself Alyce. But along with the self-esteem that comes with identity, there is also responsibility when things go wrong, and Alyce begins to doubt herself once more. Her final decision to practice midwifery and serve her apprenticeship with Jane takes into consideration both the good and the bad of the life she has chosen for herself, and her acceptance of the responsibility being placed on her.

LAYERS OF HISTORY

Each period of history has relevant children's books that delve into a specific time. Kathryn Lasky, for example, addresses witchcraft in the 17th century in *Beyond the Burning Time* (1994), with courageous Mary Chase confronting the townspeople of Salem when her mother is accused of being a witch.

Young women of the early 18th century are represented in *Calico Bush* (1931) by Rachel Field, a book that explores prejudice against someone who is different. Thirteen-year-old Marguerite Ledoux, a French girl recently arrived in America, is driven to question her identity. Marguerite's only relatives die on the trip from France to America, and she is indentured as an au pair with a New England family in a small Maine community.

The True Confessions of Charlotte Doyle (1990) by Avi features a feisty young female hero whose exploits lie within the realm of possibility but lack credibility for the time in which they occur. Females in the 19th century were not likely to sail the high seas without a chaperone, as Charlotte does, nor does it seem believable that she,

Kathryn Lasky explores the effect of the 17th-century Salem witch trials on one family in Beyond the Burning Time *(1994).*

Hitty, from Rachel Field's Hitty, Her First Hundred Years *(1928), is displayed at the Stockbridge Public Library, Stockbridge, Massachusetts. (Photographed by Carl R. Allen with permission of Polly Pierce, curator, Stockbridge Library Association)*

who has been brought up to always depend on others ("During my life I had never once—not for a moment—been without the support, the guidance, the *protection* of my elders"), would become a competent member of the crew, be accused of murder aboard ship, and be sentenced to hang. Charlotte, however, is not hanged, and she chooses to continue her independent way of life well beyond her initial ocean voyage.

Through the memoirs of a very special doll, Rachel Field takes her readers all the way through the 19th century in *Hitty: Her First Hundred Years* (1928). Hitty might be a doll, but she is definitely master of her own fate. She wisely accepts the things she cannot change and makes the best of her often bizarre experiences.

Louisa May Alcott characterized members of her own family in *Little Women* (1868); although women in the 19th century were expected to be weak, patient, timid, and subservient, Jo March and her sisters don't meet those expectations. The March sisters make it clear that they resent having to teach tiresome children, care for a fussy old lady, and spend too much of their time washing dishes and keeping things tidy. As Jo says, "It's bad enough to be a girl . . . when I like boys' games and work and manners." By making Jo a tomboy, Alcott was able to give her the traits that made heroes of men, traits that the author herself probably possessed but couldn't openly fulfill. "I'm a businessman—girl, I mean," Jo says, and Alcott, whose *Little Women* was a best-seller and who had already enjoyed financial success as a writer of gothic romances and mysteries under a pseudonym, was a businessman, too. Alcott reluctantly wrote *Little Women* at the urging of her editor, who wanted a girls' book to compete with the very popular Oliver Optic series for boys. The book was written in two parts, with the second part added when her fans demanded more stories about the March family. Alcott gave them what they wanted by having Jo get married, although Alcott herself never did marry.[1]

PIONEER WOMEN

Laura Ingalls Wilder (The Little House series), Carol Ryrie Brink (*Caddie Woodlawn*, 1935), and Patricia MacLachlan (*Sarah, Plain and Tall*, 1985) are only a few of the authors who have written about the American frontier of the late 1800s as experienced by courageous women.

In *Little House in the Big Woods* (1932), Wilder's text is simple and direct: "Once upon a time, sixty years ago, a little girl lived in the Big Woods, in a little gray house made of logs." Laura, the protagonist, is five years old and not quite as ladylike as her older sister, Mary. Even so, little girls had more freedom in the late 1800s than in the early part of that century. As Laura's mother says of times past, "It was harder for little girls. Because they had to behave like little ladies all the time, not only on Sundays. Little girls could never slide downhill, like boys. Little girls had to sit in the house and stitch on samplers."

Wilder portrays the self-sufficient Ingalls family by using historical details, and this sense of realism makes the Little House books popular year after year. Although Laura is the protagonist, all the characters, even the pet animals, become special to readers of the series, and both boys and girls become staunch Little House fans. Laura passes through adolescence into adulthood and in subsequent books marries and has children. Although Laura's family frequently faces the upheaval of moving from one homestead to another, Laura always meets new challenges with enthusiasm, excited about what might lie ahead. Wilder brings to her series the heroic actions of pioneer families through details that bring the reader directly into each scene.

> Laura and Mary listened to that lonely sound in the dark and the cold of the Big Woods, and they were not afraid. . . . They were cosy and comfortable in their little house made of logs, with the snow drifted around it and the wind crying because it could not get in by the fire.

This same attention to detail marks Carol Ryrie Brink's *Caddie Woodlawn* (1935). Caddie is a free spirit, unrestricted in her activities because her father is convinced such freedom will keep her healthy and strong. Caddie's sister Mary was less fortunate, unable to survive the harsh frontier, and her father is not about to lose another daughter. But although Caddie is healthy, she lacks the skills to be a young lady, which is sometimes uncomfortable for her. Most of the time, however, she enjoys her independence, and, when her friend Indian John and his tribe are threatened by settlers, Caddie doesn't hesitate to ride her horse straight into Indian territory to warn Indian John of the threat. Caddie's mother doesn't share Caddie's trust of Indians, but her father manages to convince the settlers not to attack. Because of Caddie's warning, the Indians and the settlers avoid an unnecessary confrontation.

When Brink wrote *Caddie Woodlawn,* which won a Newbery Medal, she wanted to celebrate American pioneer men *and* women and based Caddie's character on her own grandmother.[2] Caddie is far from representative of "sugar and spice and everything nice," but she is very much an individual, likeable and spontaneous, who cares about nature and the land and the people of the land, no matter what their color or creed. But as a reflection of the time in which this book was written, Brink felt it necessary to prepare Caddie for her future as a woman by having Father say toward the end of the book:

It's a strange thing, but somehow we expect more of girls than of boys. It's the sisters and wives and mothers, you know, Caddie, who keep the world sweet and beautiful. What a rough world it would be if there were only men and boys in it, doing things in their rough way! A woman's task is to teach them gentleness and courtesy and love and kindness.

And Brink goes on to say, "So it turned out that . . . Caddie began to learn to be a housewife."

INTO THE 20TH CENTURY

Anne Shirley, the protagonist of *Anne of Green Gables* (1908), is without a doubt one of the most popular characters in fiction. She is the creation of Canadian author Lucy Maud Montgomery, who herself demonstrates many of the traits that make up Anne's character. Both Lucy and Anne were spontaneous, imaginative, and in love with language. Both won literary accolades, and both became teachers.

But even though Montgomery used many of her own experiences in her books, Anne is her own person, and it is this individuality that appeals so much to readers. Although Anne sincerely intends to follow the guidance of her guardians, Marilla and Matthew Cuthbert, she is more apt to fall into a daydream and forget what chore she is engaged in, with disastrous results. Anne lives in a world of emotional extremes. The Cuthberts originally requested a boy to adopt, and when Anne arrives instead, Marilla's immediate thought is to send her back: The family needs a boy to help with chores and can't see any point in having a girl around. When Anne waits for Marilla to decide whether or not to keep her, she says, "I feel that I have a good deal to bear up under. It's all very well to read about sorrows and imagine yourself living through them heroically, but it's not so nice when you really come to have them, is it?" But when Anne is happy, she is unabashedly ecstatic. Anne likes giving names to flowers and trees and all manner of objects because, to her, a definite identity is very important. "You wouldn't want to be called nothing but a woman all the time," she says to Marilla.

One of the finest aspects of *Anne of Green Gables* is Anne's gradually developing maturity. Her experiences lead her to a more grounded outlook, and she is much more patient at the end of the book than at the beginning. The author thought she had come to the end of Anne's story in the first book, but her fans kept demanding more until she gave in and continued Anne's story through marriage and motherhood.

Katherine Paterson delves into the unfair treatment of young women during the Industrial Revolution with *Lyddie* (1991), set at the turn of the century. Lyddie shows her mettle from the first page of this novel as she confronts a bear that has wandered through the open door of her family's cabin. Because her father has abandoned the family and her mother is increasingly losing touch with reality, it becomes 13-year-old Lyddie's responsibility to care for her brother and two younger sisters. When she discovers how much money can be earned in the textile factories in Lowell, Massachusetts, it seems the best way for her to create some security for her family. But the hardships faced by the mill girls are more than Lyddie can tolerate, especially when her six-year-old sister Rachel, who has also been hired at the mill, develops a chronic cough; Lyddie ultimately joins the fight for change, even though it might mean forfeiting her dreams for the future.

TIMES OF TURMOIL, THE 1930s AND 1940s

The stock market crash in 1929 had repercussions that extended far beyond Wall Street in New York City. It led to the Great Depression, which affected almost everyone in the United States throughout the 1930s. In *Blue Willow* (1940), Doris Gates filters these difficult years through the viewpoint of a young girl who feels she has no real home and no security. Janey Logan, age 10, hesitates to make new friends as her family travels from farm to farm, following the crops. Each time she lets her guard down and begins to settle in, it's time to move on. But hope never really dies for Janey. When a Mexican girl Janey's age makes overtures of friendship and Janey discovers a place on the farm that looks just like the picture on her Blue Willow plate, she finds herself hoping once more that this will be the end of journeying.

Mildred Taylor in *Roll of Thunder, Hear My Cry* (1976) explores the Depression years as they affect the Logans, a Southern black family, when ownership of their land is threatened. For the Logans, the dilemma isn't finding a place to settle; it's keeping the place they have. With increasing hardship common among members of the community, both black and white, racism accelerates, and the younger members of the Logan family are suddenly faced with prejudices and misunderstandings that hadn't affected them before. Cassie Logan, independent and proud, stands up to Mr. Barnett, the white owner of Barnett Mercantile, and shortly after, to Lillian Jean Simms, who is Cassie's age but happens to be white. In both cases, Cassie is forced to compromise her feelings simply because she is black. As it becomes "more and more obvious to [her] that being black creates barriers not faced by whites,"[3] she gradually learns to outsmart her tormenters by anticipating their actions.

The Holocaust is the subject of Jane Yolen's *The Devil's Arithmetic* (1988) and Han Nolan's *If I Should Die Before I Wake* (1994) and in both books the main character, a young girl, travels back in time. In Yolen's book, Hannah/Chaya gains a better understanding of the tragedies faced by her Jewish relatives and why it's so important to remember those terrible times. Nolan takes Hilary, a neo-Nazi, back in time as Chana, a Polish Jew, who manages to survive the Holocaust. Hilary, when she returns to the present, has gained a far better understanding of what life really means to her.

Females in medieval England and Europe, in pre-Revolutionary America, in the pioneer days of 19th-century America, and during World War II—to name a few of the historical settings covered in this chapter—are everlasting role models for today's young women, and the children's books that tell the stories of these women are the legacies of their children and grandchildren.

What is history to the children of today? Stories about World War II and the Holocaust, about the Gulf War, about recent presidential elections, would all be historical events to a contemporary child. Each generation of children will have a longer stretch of history and a far greater collection of facts to learn. A young woman with a strong base in reading historical novels can discover for herself the contributions made by women over the years and can choose her own heroes to emulate.

NOTES

1. Marjorie N. Allen. *100 Years of Children's Books in America: Decade by Decade.* New York: Facts On File, 1996, pp. 8, 89.
2. Ibid, p. 79.
3. Ibid, p. 243.

ANNOTATED BIBLIOGRAPHY

Alcott, Louisa May. *Little Women.* Boston: Little, Brown, 1868 (first half), 1869 (second half); New York: Scholastic, 1986. (Middle Reading)

> The March family chronicles were based largely on Alcott's own family, with all its faults and failures. The four sisters—Meg, Jo, Beth, and Amy—are sharply drawn characters from the first page of this classic novel. Jo, tomboy and nonconformist, is the protagonist; the personalities of her three sisters, plus mother, father, and the boy next door, Laurie Lawrence, revolve around and contribute to Jo's personal growth throughout the novel.

Avi. *The True Confessions of Charlotte Doyle.* New York: Orchard Books, 1990. (Middle Reading)

> Charlotte travels from England to America unchaperoned, an unlikely circumstance for a young woman raised to depend on others. Perhaps because of her innocence, she shows poor judgment by defending the disagreeable Captain Jaggery, skipper of the *Seahawk,* during an incident aboard ship. Her actions cause the crew to turn against her, and she struggles to regain their good will in the second half of the book. Captain Jaggery then accuses her of murdering Mr. Hollybrass, the first mate, and she is tried before her shipmates, found guilty, and sentenced to be hanged. Fortunately, however, both she and the crew discover the truth about Mr. Hollybrass's murder, and in the end the right person is punished for the deed.

Blos, Joan W. *A Gathering of Days: A New England Girl's Journal, 1830–32.* New York: Scribner, 1979; New York: Aladdin, 1990. NEWBERY MEDAL. (Middle Reading)

> This story is written in a diary format by teenager Catherine Hall. Her experiences enlighten the reader about the difficulties faced by New England pioneers in the early 1830s. Catherine's mother died of a fever when Catherine was nine, and she has taken on the responsibility of caring and cooking for her father and her younger sister, Matty. When her father remarries, Catherine at first cannot bring herself to refer to her father's wife as anything but "she," but gradually the two begin to warm

to each other. Catherine refuses to call her "mother," but finally agrees to call her "Mammann," a combination of Mama and Ann, her stepmother's name. Catherine's days are spent at school or doing chores at home, with only occasional moments of frivolity. Life for pioneer women in the 1830s was simple but hard, and death was a common occurrence—a truth Catherine has already discovered and must face again when her best friend, Cassie, dies suddenly.

Brink, Carol Ryrie. *Caddie Woodlawn*. New York: Macmillan, 1935; New York: Aladdin, 1990. NEWBERY MEDAL. (Middle Reading)

When the Woodlawn family moves from Boston to Wisconsin, both Caddie and her sister Mary are frail. When little Mary dies, Caddie's father is determined that Caddie will not follow the same fate. He allows her the freedom to run wild with her brothers, and she becomes brown and strong and healthy. But even on the frontier, girls are supposed to behave with restraint, and visitors are somewhat shocked at 11-year-old Caddie's behavior. Caddie is torn between her desire to please her parents by behaving well and her desire to act freely, but she cannot help being more spontaneous than reserved. Fortunately for everyone, she makes the decision to face danger in order to avert a confrontation between the settlers and the nearby Indian tribe when a misunderstanding occurs.

Cushman, Karen. *The Midwife's Apprentice*. New York: Clarion, 1995. NEWBERY MEDAL. (Middle Reading)

The story takes place in medieval times with Brat, a girl who becomes Beetle and then finally Alyce, each new identity taking her self-esteem one step higher. She is a homeless child, perhaps 12 or 13 years of age, who has, ever since she can remember, been responsible for her own survival and makes the best of the opportunities that arise. Being taken in and apprenticed to the midwife Jane Sharp insures that she has enough food to eat and that she no longer has to sleep in a dung heap, but even when she accepts herself as Alyce, things don't always go right. She has to learn that early success in midwifery can turn to tragedy at another time, and it is the midwife who is blamed when such a thing happens. But Alyce shows her strength when hardship comes, and with the companionship of her cat Purr manages to overcome adversity and decide to take the bad with the good as a midwife's apprentice.

Field, Rachel. *Calico Bush*. New York: Macmillan, 1931; New York: Yearling, 1990. (Middle Reading)

In 1743 Marguerite Ledoux leaves prerevolutionary France and sails with her Grand-mere and Oncle Pierre to settle in the community of Marlboro, but when her only two relatives die of fever, she must travel to the rugged Maine coast with the Sargent family as an au pair. Because she is dark where the Sargents are fair, because she is French while they are of Scottish stock, because she is Catholic and they are Protestant, because she is so different from the others, Marguerite is looked upon in the settlement as suspect. But when Mr. Sargent is seriously injured, it is Marguerite who bravely faces the Indians and manages to avert a violent confrontation.

————. *Hitty: Her First Hundred Years.* Illus. Dorothy Lathrop. New York: Macmillan, 1929; New York: Yearling, 1990. NEWBERY MEDAL. (Middle Reading)

Hitty may be a doll, but one of her finest qualities is her ability to adjust to any situation, no matter how difficult or how uncomfortable. Hitty just never gives up. Her adventures take her through 100 years of American history as she travels through New England, heads out to sea as passenger in a ship and is inadvertently lost overboard, is worshiped as a goddess on a South Sea island, spends time in India, lands back in America at the Carolinas, goes to Philadelphia, lives with Quakers, becomes a dressmaker's model, and eventually returns to New England.

Frank, Anne. *Anne Frank: The Diary of a Young Girl.* New York: Doubleday, 1952; New York: Bantam, 1993. (Middle Reading)

As a reminder of the atrocities against 6 million Jews in World War II, the courage of Anne Frank, who in her diary shows that she is like any adolescent, is a beacon that keeps that time in history alive. Anne was 13 when she started her diary and 15 when she died in the concentration camp at Bergen-Belsen.

Gates, Doris. *Blue Willow.* New York: Viking, 1940; New York: Puffin, 1976. (Middle Reading)

Janey Larkin doesn't know what it's like to dwell in one place and to have a house like the one on the Blue Willow plate she cherishes. Her family just manages to get by as itinerant workers, traveling from one place to another, looking for new crops to gather. When Janey meets Lupe, whose family are also itinerants, she hesitates to accept Lupe's friendship, but when Janey's mother becomes ill and the family isn't able to travel on, she gives in to her desire for companionship. Unfortunately, by not leaving when the crops are in, the Larkins are running out of money, and Janey gives up her beloved plate as insurance for the rent they owe. "It takes courage to live the way we do without losing your grip on things," her father had said, and Janey remembers those words and finds the courage to keep hoping. It is because of her love for the precious plate that she is finally brave enough to confront the owner of the property and discovers that it is not the owner but his foreman who has made their lives so miserable.

Konigsburg, E. L. *A Proud Taste for Scarlet and Miniver.* New York: Atheneum, 1973; New York: Yearling, 1985. (Middle Reading)

Although this book covers court life in the Middle Ages, it also has the elements of a fantasy. Eleanor of Aquitaine is waiting in Heaven for the love of her life, her second husband Henry II, to be sent to her from Hell. As she waits, those who have been closest to her and are also in Heaven tell Eleanor's story, each from his or her own viewpoint, and in the telling, describe Eleanor's character and her family's influence on history.

Lasky, Kathryn. *Beyond the Burning Time.* New York: Blue Sky Press, 1994. (Young Adult)

Twelve-year-old Mary Chase is horrified when other girls her own age begin having seizures and behaving violently, saying they are bedeviled, and when Mary's mother dismisses the girls' actions as contrived, Mary is frightened that her mother will be accused of witchcraft. For some reason, it is the most pious women in the community who are being accused and taken off to prison after being condemned by the young girls as the cause of their seizures. Finally Goody Chase is indeed accused and taken away in chains. It is up to Mary to find a way to save her mother before she is hanged. During the first part of this novel, multiple viewpoints may cause confusion for some readers, but the second half of the book, told from the viewpoint of Mary Chase, builds in suspense and portrays the Salem witch trials as they truly happened.

MacLachlan, Patricia. *Sarah, Plain and Tall.* New York: Harper, 1985. NEWBERY MEDAL. (Middle Reading)

The author draws upon a story of her own family in the latter years of the 19th century, when a widower with two children advertises for a mail-order bride to join him on the prairie. Sarah, who describes herself in her letter as plain and tall, comes to marry Anna and Caleb's father, Jacob, and young Anna not only must deal with a new stepmother but must also finally deal with her mother's death, which happened right after Caleb was born. This exquisitely sculpted novel uses only enough words to build emotion and leave the reader with an indelible memory of the story.

Montgomery, Lucy Maud. *Anne of Green Gables.* Boston: L. C. Page, 1908; New York: Scholastic, 1989. (Middle Reading)

Anne Shirley, abandoned orphan, is taken in by the taciturn Matthew Cuthbert and his no-nonsense sister, Marilla, against Marilla's better judgment. Marilla can't help but be charmed by the exuberant Anne, and Matthew immediately finds her captivating. Anne's spontaneity makes her totally unpredictable, and Marilla despairs of ever making a lady of her. But Anne also learns from her mistakes, and by the end of the book, she develops into a determined but more sensible young woman.

Nolan, Han. *If I Should Die Before I Wake.* San Diego: Harcourt Brace, 1994. (Young Adult)

In this powerful novel, Nolan introduces an angry young woman of the 1990s who suddenly finds herself in the past with a different identity. Hilary, a neo-Nazi initiate, has been seriously injured in an accident and awakens in a Jewish hospital. She has a head injury and drifts in and out of consciousness, traveling from the present to the past each time she loses consciousness. Even as she reverts to taking on the persona of Chana, a 13-year-old Jewish girl who lives with her family in a Polish ghetto during World War II, a part of her stays connected to the present and observes her Jewish self with disdain. However, as she continues in Chana's world and is introduced to the horrors of the Holocaust, she gradually begins to cherish Chana's loving family, almost regretting consciousness and the lack of love she has experienced in her dysfunctional contemporary life. As the past and the present begin to merge, Hilary/Chana must decide between life and death and whether she will rise above self for the sake of others.

Paterson, Katherine. *Lyddie.* New York: Lodestar, 1991. (Young Adult)

When Lyddie discovers the amount of money she can make by working in the mills, she leaves home. She regrets having to go because her mother is mentally unstable and her younger siblings will no longer have Lyddie to care for them, but the need for money for the family is stronger than Lyddie's feelings. Life in the mills is grueling and often dangerous, but Lyddie avoids becoming involved with the other girls, who are making an effort to defy management, because she doesn't want to lose her job. When her mother is institutionalized and her younger sister becomes Lyddie's responsibility, the only way she can keep her sister with her is to have her work at the mill. But Rachel is frail, and when she shows signs of illness with the chronic cough that often is the result of mill work, Lyddie realizes that loved ones and friends take precedence over money.

Taylor, Mildred. *Roll of Thunder, Hear My Cry.* New York: Dial, 1976; New York: Puffin, 1993. NEWBERY MEDAL. (Middle Reading)

Cassie Logan, a young Southern black girl, has been raised to take pride in herself and her family. It isn't until the Great Depression causes her family to lose status in their community, with the children becoming the victims of prejudice and condescension, that Cassie learns that she must hold back her true feelings in a community ruled by whites.

Wilder, Laura Ingalls. *Little House in the Big Woods.* New York: Harper, 1932, 1993. (Early Reading)

The charm of this ever-popular series lies in the author's detailed descriptions of life in Wisconsin in the 1870s. The members of the Ingalls family are close knit and hard working, with Ma the practical member of the family and Pa the one who takes time out to share storytelling and his lively violin playing with his daughters, Mary, Laura, and baby Carrie. The life they lead is simple but secure, and the descriptions of how the family prepares for the winter by making the most of everything they grow and hunt creates a detailed picture of life in the wilderness. There is danger, with wild bears and boars and the chance of being lost in the Big Woods, but the girls are brought up to confront danger when it comes, even as they learn the niceties of needlepoint and quilt-making.

Yolen, Jane. *The Devil's Arithmetic.* New York: Viking, 1988. (Young Adult)

Hannah/Chaya, a 13-year-old Jewish girl of the 1980s, travels back in time when she symbolically opens the door for Elijah during first night's seder. Unlike author Han Nolan's Hilary, Hannah is part of a close-knit family. Like Hilary, she is embarrassed by her relatives and separates herself from them. It is annoying to her that members of her family keep bringing up events that happened long ago during World War II, and it isn't until she is transported back to a Jewish village in Poland during that time that she experiences firsthand the horrors of the Holocaust and begins to understand why it's important not to forget.

4

EAST IS EAST AND WEST IS WEST: IDENTIFYING SELF

I think that stories are the very heart of our civilization and culture. . . . we can make sure that the kind of stories our children read carry something of the aura of the tales our mothers and sisters told us.

—Chinua Achebe,
in *Pipers at the Gates of Dawn: The Wisdom of Children's Literature* by Jonathan Cott

The ability to communicate via Internet allows for immediate connections among the countries of the world. It is important for American children to grow up understanding their neighbors at home and abroad, as it is equally important for the children of other countries to understand American culture, which is not the melting pot that people thought it would be. There seems to be, instead, in the latter years of the 20th century, an increased tendency for ethnic groups to remain separate from one another.

In other countries, translated editions of American children's books are as much a part of their literature as the children's book collections of their own countries. Very few international children's books, however, are translated into English and made part of America's collections. Even the books from Great Britain, when published in America, are often revised to substitute familiar American words for English words—such as *diapers* for *nappies,* or *trucks* for *lorries.* The editorial concern, especially with fiction, is that unless foreign books are "Americanized," they won't be popular with young readers who want the language in their fiction easy to understand.[1]

Often, however, by naturalizing foreign texts for American children, cultural differences are homogenized and the diversity of language obscured.

In scrutinizing children's books about different cultures, three separate categories become immediately evident: books by American authors writing about cultures foreign to them, books by American authors writing about cultures indigenous to them, and books by foreign authors published first in their country, then translated for a North American readership.

In the early years of the 20th century, children's books that portrayed different cultures were often written by authors who had no ties to those cultures and little true understanding of different ways of life. Books about Eastern cultures portrayed Western world values, and too often, African-American characters were stereotypes or caricatures. Books about other cultures took "a 'tourist' approach, stressing the exotic or presenting a static society with simple categories."[2]

In the past 20 years, however, writers and publishers have made an effort to enlighten readers by presenting the emotional viewpoint of characters within a culture, characters from the inside looking out rather than from the outside looking in. Fran Leeper

Buss enlisted the aid of Daisy Cubias to present an El Salvadoran viewpoint in *Journey of the Sparrows* (1991). British author Susan Cooper, who divides her time between England and the United States, offered a character steeped in ancient Scottish folklore who uses a high-tech computer as a means of traveling from Scotland to Canada, in *The Boggart* (1993). And Virginia Hamilton has celebrated African-American roots in all of her fiction.

BREAKING THE MOLD

Swedish author Astrid Lindgren, creator of the irrepressible Pippi Longstocking (see page 119), offers humor and pathos in *Ronia, the Robber's Daughter* (1981; translated from the Swedish in 1983), a turnabout of the male rite of passage. Instead of the classic male hero setting out on a quest, it is Ronia, a female, who must make it on her own. Instead of a boy transferring his loyalty from his mother to his mate, it is Ronia who decides to transfer her loyalty from her father to Birk, the son of a rival robber. Lindgren makes real the imaginary as Ronia faces the threat of the Flying Harpies, Gray Dwarfs, and the Unearthly Ones when she runs away from home with Birk and lives in a cave. But Ronia's determination and bravery bring about a confrontation with her father and test her mettle as nothing has done before.

In order to evaluate female identity as it relates to culture, it's important to understand the social structure and roles of men and women in different countries. Bette Bao Lord's *In the Year of the Boar and Jackie Robinson* (1984) expresses in humorous but revealing terms the difficulties of a young girl who chooses the American name Shirley Temple as she tries to adjust from the Chinese way of life, in which women are expected to be submissive and stay in the background, to the strange customs of American culture as interpreted by Chinese immigrants. In China, Confucianism traditionally defined the place of a woman. As noted by historian Ronald Takaki, "She was instructed to obey her father as a daughter, her husband as a wife, and her eldest son as a widow."[3] In America, Chinese and American customs are likely to mix.

In Chunking, Shirley's well-to-do family took servants for granted. When Shirley's mother asks Father where the cook is in their tiny

American apartment, Father says, "In America, all cooks work in restaurants. In America," Father continues, "the wife cooks." Since Shirley's mother has never expressed any interest in preparing food, Shirley is convinced they will starve. But she finds benefits to living in America—for instance, canned food that requires no preparation.

As Shirley adjusts to the odd customs of America and settles into a routine in her Brooklyn school, she makes an important discovery. Here, she doesn't have to "wait for gray hairs to be considered wise. Here, she could speak up, question even the conduct of the President. Here, Shirley Temple Wong was somebody." The crowning glory for Shirley is being chosen to present the key of her school, P.S. 8, to her hero, baseball star Jackie Robinson, whose accomplishments have opened the door for her to be whomever she wants to be. Regardless of a reader's ethnicity, this is a book that confirms the opportunities open to any young woman who has been brought up to believe in herself.

One of the difficulties for Asian females is the American belief that young women in Eastern countries are oppressed against their will and need someone to rescue them. Another is the belief among many Americans that all Asian cultures are the same. Both beliefs are wrong. Many Asian women accept with pleasure their roles as matriarchs of the family, controlling financial and household affairs; many also take great pride in their native country's heritage, which means different things to the Japanese, the Chinese, or the Koreans. Two books with a Japanese setting, *Little Sister* (1996) by Kara Dalkey and *Shizuko's Daughter* (1993) by Kyoko Mori, take the reader from ancient Japan in the first to contemporary Japan in the second and offer a better understanding of Japanese culture and its ties to the past.

Suzanne Fisher Staples, a United Press International correspondent who spent several years in Pakistan, was disturbed by the status of women there and decided she could best inform others about the universality of the human condition by writing fiction for young people.[4] The result was *Shabanu* (1989), one of the first children's books written about Islamic culture. *Shabanu* is the story of a Cholistani girl who comes of age in a desert community. At age 11, Shabanu takes for granted her approaching arranged marriage and, in fact, is rather pleased with her father's choice for her. But when her older sister's fiancé is killed, Shabanu loses her mate to her sister and finds herself promised to an older man—all decided by the

Bette Bao Lord's In the Year of the Boar and Jackie Robinson *(1984) introduces Shirley Temple Wong, a young girl whose family has moved from
China to New York.*

father for the good of the family. The positive message in this story is Shabanu's belief in herself and her ability to deal with her fate and hold on to her personal identity.

DISSOLVING THE COLOR BARRIER

When the first slaves were transported to America, they were members of an African tribal culture with their own traditions and language. But they weren't allowed to retain their traditions or language; they were forced to speak English without any formal education, and they were prohibited from learning how to read. Over the years, before slavery ended in the United States, an African-American culture evolved, with frequent interbreeding between white masters and slaves. Skin color rather than cultural origins became the factor that divided "blacks" and "whites." Today, many Americans with an African heritage are interested in learning about the traditions of Africa, but many also see themselves primarily as Americans.

Of course, not all black people have a direct African heritage. Identifying someone by cultural heritage rather than skin color opens up a whole different viewpoint, a different way of seeing someone. Malcolm Bosse features two young people from Borneo in *Deep Dream of the Rain Forest* (1993), and Frances Temple, who lived in Haiti and cared deeply about the fate of the Haitian people, wrote of their struggles in *Taste of Salt: A Story of Modern Haiti* (1992). When Virginia Hamilton celebrates African pride in *Zeely* (1967) and Native American pride in *Arilla Sun Down* (1976), she is saying, "Look at me. This is who I am."

Zeely features a young black girl, Elizabeth, who is convinced she has discovered an African princess on her uncle's farm. In the process of getting to know tall, dignified, and proud Zeely Tayber, Elizabeth, who calls herself "Geeder," finds that Zeely has no royal blood but takes pride in who she is, even if that means taking care of her father's hogs.

Books for older readers tend to delve more deeply into the search for identity. The main theme in Hamilton's *Arilla Sun Down* and in a recently published book titled *The Last Rainmaker* (1997), by Sherry Garland, is the treatment of Native Americans in the American West. In each case, the leading protagonist is female. In

VIRGINIA HAMILTON

He has always
been the
perfect one.
How can
she compete
with perfection?

Arilla Sun Down

The main character in Virginia Hamilton's Arilla Sun Down *(1976) must come to terms with her mixed heritage.*

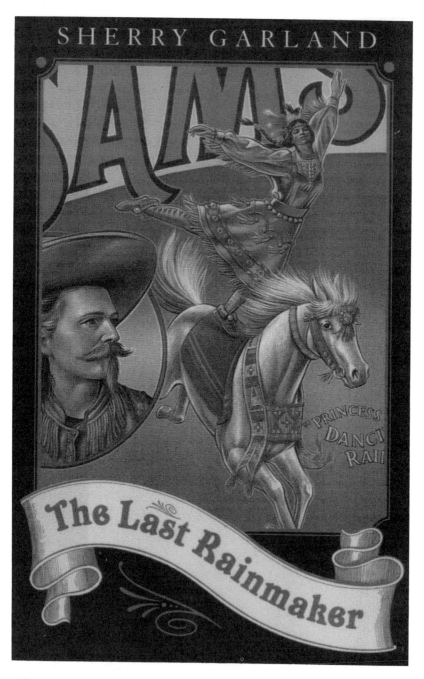

The Last Rainmaker *(1997) by Sherry Garland explores the treatment of Native Americans in the American West through one girl's search for identity.*

each case, the main character is of mixed heritage. Arilla's problem is lack of self-esteem, and she sees her brother, Jack, as far more important than she. He is self-confident and apparently comfortable with his identity. Jack's physical appearance negates his African-American genealogy, and he identifies himself as Amerind. For Arilla, the choice is more complicated. Although she and Jack share the same bloodlines, Arilla's features and coloring label her African American rather than Native American, and she cannot ignore her mixed heritage. Caroline Long in *Rainmaker* discovers that she is Wichita and white and that her mother, who died when she was born, was a featured performer in a Wild West show. She begins a quest to find out more about her heritage.

STRENGTH OF CHARACTER

The common thread through the stories discussed in this chapter is the growing strength of each of the female protagonists as she meets and overcomes obstacles to her development. *Julie of the Wolves*, (1972) by Jean Craighead George and *Island of the Blue Dolphins* (1960) by Scott O'Dell are award-winning books that feature females as heroes and did so long before it was the popular thing to do. No matter how a particular culture defines female identity—*Julie* is set in Alaska and *Blue Dolphins*, in the South Pacific—as long as a girl manages to avoid becoming a victim, as long as she retains her own identity and refuses to compromise her inner self, she will remain strong and will lead a full and satisfying existence.

The qualities that give a woman the ability to overcome adversity and achieve her goals are developed through belief in one's potential. The female protagonists discussed in this chapter are all strong characters, regardless of the social expectations or the perceived role of women in their particular culture.

NOTES
1. Jane Whitehead. "'This Is *Not* What I Wrote!': The Americanization of British Children's Books—Part I." *The Horn Book Magazine*, November/December 1996, pp. 687–693.
2. Betsy Hearne and Roger Sutton, eds. *Evaluating Children's Books: A*

Critical Look. Champaign: University of Illinois at Urbana-Champaign, Graduate School of Library and Information Science, 1993, p. 140.
3. Ronald Takaki. *A Different Mirror: A History of Multicultural America.* Boston: Little, Brown, 1994, p. 209.
4. Maryclare O'Donnell Himmel. "Staples, Suzanne Fisher." In *Children's Books and Their Creators: An Invitation to the Feast of Twentieth-century Children's Literature,* edited by Anita Silvey. Boston: Houghton Mifflin, 1995, p. 624.

ANNOTATED BIBLIOGRAPHY

Bosse, Malcolm. *Deep Dream of the Rain Forest.* New York: Farrar, Straus & Giroux, 1993. (Young Adult)

> This story reflects the respect in which girls are held in the Iban tribe of Borneo, as Bayan and his female cohort, Tambong, embark on a quest commanded by a dream. The two decide they must kidnap a white English boy, Harry Windsor, who becomes the catalyst that helps their dream come true and guides all three into a rite of passage.

Buss, Fran Leeper. *Journey of the Sparrows.* With Daisy Cubias. New York: Penguin, 1991. (Young Adult)

> María at 15 is self-conscious about her developing body, but she has led a sheltered life in El Salvador. When her country undergoes upheaval and becomes unsafe, she and her family must make their way out. As they attempt to cross the border into the United States, María's feelings about Tomás, the boy who is traveling with them, are submerged by fear of being caught by soldiers before they can cross the U.S. border. María's story, which should be that of a young woman on the verge of maturity learning to deal with her own sexuality, is compounded by the threat to herself, her pregnant sister, her small brother, her mother and younger sister, who remain in Mexico, and her father, who may not have survived. Their experiences, so different from those of America's middle-class teenagers, is an enlightening saga in which the mere fact of being alive is enough to offer hope for the future.

Choi, Sook Nyul. *Year of Impossible Goodbyes.* Boston: Houghton Mifflin, 1991. (Middle Reading)

> Nine-year-old Sookan is proud of her Korean heritage and resents the presence of the Japanese troops and their leader, Captain Narita, who insists that the villagers learn the Japanese language and adopt a belief system other than their

own. She watches her grandfather die three days after Captain Narita orders her grandfather's special pine tree to be chopped down; she watches the girls from the sock factory being transferred to the front, where they must suffer a fate that seems worse than death. Through it all, she has the support of her courageous mother. But when World War II finally comes to an end and the Russians take over, the oppression is too overwhelming and Sookan's family tries to escape to South Korea, where they will be free. This is when Sookan is separated from her mother and must rely on her own strength to take her brother and herself across the border.

Dalkey, Kara. *Little Sister.* San Diego: Harcourt, Brace, 1996. (Middle Reading)

The protagonist, 13-year-old Mitsuko, in this story of 12th-century Heian Japan, shows herself to be brave and determined when tragedy strikes her family and she is cast from a life of ease as a member of the nobility to fighting for survival in the Japanese countryside. The story employs all the elements of storytelling in ancient Japan—mythology, folk tales, Buddhism, and Shintoism—along with details of life in the city of Heian-kyo during the reign of the Fujiwara family. This book, with its historical detail and traditional stories, allows young people a better understanding of Japanese culture.

Garland, Sherry. *The Last Rainmaker.* San Diego: Harcourt Brace, 1997. (Young Adult)

This is a story of a young woman, Caroline Long, who suddenly discovers at age 13 that she is part Native American. Instead of allowing Caroline to find her own unique identity, however, Garland places her in a position where she must make the choice to be either white or Indian. This dilemma does more to lengthen the gap between Anglo-Saxon Americans and native peoples than to create understanding and harmony between races. The author's effort to illustrate the unfair treatment of Native Americans over the years tends to sacrifice character development.

George, Jean Craighead. *Julie of the Wolves.* Illus. John Schoenherr. New York: Harper, 1972, 1974. NEWBERY MEDAL. (Young Adult)

Miyax lives on the tundra and yearns to visit San Francisco where her pen pal, Amy, lives. Amy calls Miyax "Julie," and Miyax/Julie is torn between her native culture and American culture, which seems to offer so much freedom. When Julie becomes a victim of violence in her arranged marriage to a local boy, she runs away, intending to go to San Francisco, but she becomes lost on the tundra. Her survival depends on her own instincts and the lessons her father taught her about nature. When she meets up with a pack of wolves, she instinctively communicates with them and manages to survive.

Hamilton, Virginia. *Arilla Sun Down.* New York: Macmillan, 1976; New York: Scholastic, 1995. (Young Adult)

Hamilton shows herself to be a genius with words as she develops this coming-of-age novel about 12-year-old Arilla, whose mixed blood sets her apart from other people in her small Midwestern community. Arilla comes full circle in her struggle to discover her true identity in this thoughtful study of family relationships and the love/hate relationship that exists between a brother and sister, a relationship that reaches a mature balance by the end of the book.

———. *Zeely.* New York: Macmillan, 1967; New York: Aladdin, 1993. (Middle Reading)

Elizabeth Perry lives in her imagination, and when she and her brother visit her uncle's farm and she catches a glimpse of the regal Zeely, six feet tall and resembling the picture Elizabeth has of a Watusi queen in Africa, she wants to believe that Zeely is royalty. But when she becomes acquainted with Zeely, she discovers that her idol, though descended from an African Watusi tribe, has no royal blood. Zeely helps her father with the hogs and takes pride in fulfilling her responsibilities. Through her friendship with Zeely, Elizabeth learns to accept her own identity and to believe in herself.

Lindgren, Astrid. *Ronia, the Robber's Daughter.* Trans. Patricia Crompton. New York: Viking, 1983; New York: Puffin, 1985. (Middle Reading)

Robin Hood, who stole from the rich and gave to the poor, is looked upon as a hero. Matt, a robber chieftain who lives in a stronghold at the top of a mountain in Sweden, falsely claims he too steals from the rich and gives to the poor when his small daughter, Ronia, asks him why he takes what belongs to others. The story, a reflection on Scandinavian culture, presents romance in a pristine setting with friendship the overriding force. As Ronia matures, she ventures into the forest and eventually meets Dirk, the son of a rival robber baron. Ronia and Dirk, standing by their principles, both represent the definition of hero without regard for gender.

Lord, Betty Bao. *In the Year of the Boar and Jackie Robinson.* New York: Harper, 1984, 1986. (Middle Reading)

When young Bandit discovers she will travel with her mother from China to Brooklyn, New York, after her father sends for them, she is more excited than apprehensive. Although their life changes drastically—her mother, who has always depended on servants, must now take on the household chores—it is good for the family to be together, and Bandit, now known as Shirley Temple Wong, relies on her strength of character to adjust to the unusual expectations of American adults in a society far different from that in Chunking. Her first dilemma comes when she gives her age as 10 and is put into fifth grade instead of fourth grade where she belongs. (In China a child is one year old at birth, and Shirley is unaware that this is not the case in America.) Although Lord doesn't focus directly on attitudes toward females in China and America, Shirley clearly feels good about herself within her family, in her community, and among her schoolmates, and the story suggests that her positive outlook is a product of her upbringing in China.

Mori, Kyoko. *Shizuko's Daughter*. New York: Henry Holt, 1993. (Young Adult)

In this story set in contemporary Japan, 12-year-old Yuki must deal with the unexpected suicide of her mother, Shizuko. Her adjustment is made more difficult by Japanese tradition. When Yuki's father remarries and Yuki asks to go to Tokyo to stay with her aunt, she is not allowed to do so because people might think her father and stepmother are neglecting her. Yuki must make her rite of passage on her own, until her grandmother Masa, mother of Shizuko, helps her understand how to deal with her altered life.

O'Dell, Scott. *Island of the Blue Dolphins*. Boston: Houghton Mifflin, 1960; New York: Yearling, 1987. NEWBERY MEDAL. (Middle Reading)

On an isolated Pacific island a 12-year-old native girl, Karana, enjoys her peaceful routine, watching the blue dolphins frolic and otters play, as she participates in the life of her village. But when the Russian captain of an Aleut ship shows his dishonest nature, tragedy follows. Karana's father is killed by one of the Aleut hunters and the captain flees with his ship, but not before many of the island men lose their lives. This leads to a new distribution of duties, with many women taking on hunting duties for the first time. The life of the tribe is so disrupted that the people decide to leave the island. But Karana's small brother is inadvertently left behind when the villagers start to leave, and Karana jumps into the cove to rescue him. This is the beginning of Karana's fight for survival, alone on the island when her brother is killed and seemingly without hope for rescue.

Staples, Suzanne Fisher. *Shabanu*. New York: Alfred A. Knopf, 1989. (Young Adult)

Although 11-year-old Shabanu rebels against the decisions made on her behalf by her father, she must in the long run accept her fate. When her sister, Phulan, whose fiancé has been killed, marries a man originally promised to Shabanu, her father arranges a marriage for her with a man old enough to be her grandfather, the wealthy Rahim-sahib. In Pakistani culture, a young woman is not allowed the freedom to choose her mate, but Shabanu, unlike her docile sister, never allows her inner identity to be absorbed by male dominance.

Temple, Frances. *Taste of Salt: A Story of Modern Haiti*. New York: HarperCollins, 1992. (Young Adult)

Temple portrays male and female courage equally in this story of two young people: Djo, who suffers terrible burns when the military junta burn down the orphanage where he lives, and Jeremie, the young woman who cares for him and believes, along with Djo, in the ability of the Reverend Jean-Bertrand Aristide to free Haiti from oppression. The story is told from the viewpoint of both Djo and Jeremie, each of whom has suffered tragic circumstances.

Watkins, Yoko Kawishima. *So Far from the Bamboo Grove*. New York: Lothrop, Lee & Shepard, 1986. (Young Adult)

Where *Year of Impossible Goodbyes* (see pages 80–81) avoids specific details of Japanese cruelty and inhuman treatment of the Korean people, Watkins describes these acts in detail, based on her own experiences as a Japanese child in Korea during and after World War II. Her descriptions of the chaos caused when the Communists moved into North Korea and the danger she and her family faced because they were Japanese are uncompromising. In their efforts to escape to South Korea they are on the verge of starvation and watch people die daily, including their own mother. Watkins makes it clear that Japanese cruelty was not a racial trait but was limited to individuals who were as unacceptable to her as they were to Koreans.

5

ISSUES IN ADOLESCENCE: ACCEPTING SELF

Reading is a means of thinking with another person's mind; it forces you to stretch your own.

—Charles Scribner, Jr., publisher

Children's literature gives young people an inside track on the emotions of adolescence. Books are a way to face grief, deal with perceived differences, and gain self-confidence. When written well, they create empathy and understanding at a time when young people are trying to adjust to the unexpected complexities of growing up.

Unfortunately, in many of the books that focus more on social issues than character development, the "problem" takes over the story, and the story as a whole suffers. Since the 1970s, many books have addressed just about every issue in modern society, but only a few have exhibited sufficient complexity to remain in print.

BREAKING WITH TABOOS

In 1972 Norma Klein's *Mom, the Wolfman, and Me* heralded a series of young adult novels that flaunted previous taboos in children's books. Brett, age 11, lives with her mother, who has never been married, and this apparent disregard for convention makes Brett the scapegoat of derision. In the 1990s fewer people look askance at an unmarried mother, but when Klein wrote this story, it was socially unacceptable to have a child out of wedlock. The words *illegitimacy* and *unwed mother* carried a stigma that set a child apart in more conventional settings. Although some accused Klein of sensationalism, others were more accepting of the matter-of-fact protagonist. Through the book Klein implies that if Brett can be so casual about her mother having intercourse without being married, then there's no reason for readers and librarians to get upset about it, either.[1]

It is difficult enough for young people to make their way through adolescence, but when they have additional adjustments to make because of physical or mental obstacles or feel alienated from their peers because they see themselves as different, they become easily discouraged. Knowing that others share the same challenges and have managed to rise above them takes away much of the anxiety associated with unwanted isolation.

At the young adult level, it is difficult to find a novel that addresses relationships between two males or between two females in a way that takes such relationships for granted. For so long, homosexuality has been ignored as a way of life, but many of today's young people look at such a life as normal for those who live it.

One book that has managed to rise above the ordinary is *Annie on My Mind* (1982) by Nancy Garden. The book is a thoughtful character study of a girl from an ultraconservative environment who is confused by her strong feelings for another girl. When 17-year-old Eliza Winthrop meets Annie Kenyon at the Metropolitan Museum of Art in New York City, she knows immediately that this is a girl she wants to know better. Annie is spontaneous, whereas Eliza is subdued; imaginative, whereas Eliza is practical; and independent, whereas Eliza is bound by her obligations to others. Before long it is obvious that the two young women complete each other, socially and sexually, but Eliza must find the courage to be true to herself in the face of overwhelming disapproval from her family and society. There are no easy answers in this book, but the satisfactory resolution keeps hope alive.

Francesca Lia Block writes about contemporary young people living in a highly imaginative West Coast setting, and the nontraditional characters in her stories accept each other without bias. The novel *Weetzie Bat* (1989) portrays young people in a manner that contradicts the social tenets taken for granted in America before the book was published. Weetzie Bat is an adolescent whose parents are divorced. Her father lives in New York, and her mother lives in Los Angeles. Weetzie Bat lives independently from both parents in a commune-type setting. Her roommates are Dirk and Duck, two young gay men, and Secret Agent Lover Man, who suddenly appears in her life when a genie grants her wish. The reaction to this book has been mixed, with some people appreciating the honest portrait of a community of young adults whose rebellious parents grew up during the 1960s. Others are concerned about the apparent approval of teenage sexual relations and a bohemian lifestyle.[2] Some public and school librarians have refused to carry Block's books, but most young adult librarians leave the choices up to their young patrons.

Block is a young writer from southern California who focuses on this region of the United States from a contemporary viewpoint.

Her books are part reality and part fantasy, and her characters seem to take for granted a life that is unorthodox at the very least: As the title character says, "I don't know about happily ever after . . . but I know about happily." Block is a compelling writer, and her portraits of young people who are more responsible than their parents are enlightening at a time in social history when the family unit is in a state of flux. *Weetzie Bat* is a book that lends itself to discussion between parent and child.

In *Witch Baby* (1991), sequel to *Weetzie Bat,* Weetzie's friend Duck visits his family in New Mexico with his companion, Dirk. When Witch Baby, who has traveled with them, reveals to Duck's mother that her son is gay, Duck must face his family's initial rejection. Witch Baby was taken in by Weetzie Bat and her Secret Agent Lover Man when she was an infant. She believes she is an abandoned child and is unaware that Secret Agent Lover Man is her true father. Because she is convinced she doesn't belong anywhere, she finds it difficult to accept love and continually tries to prove she is not worthy of it, causing pain for herself and others. But in this novel, understanding eventually prevails, even for Witch Baby.

In the 1990s, few taboos remain regarding subject matter in children's books, but the treatment of a particular issue makes some books stand above the others. In *I Am an Artichoke* (1995) by Lucy Frank, the narrator is 15-year-old Sarah, who is hired as a mother's helper in New York City for the summer. Sarah gradually discovers that both 12-year-old Emily and Emily's mother, Florence, are obsessive about food. Florence is on a perpetual diet but goes on eating binges when she is upset; Emily eats little and exercises constantly. Emily fits the profile for the so-called typical adolescent suffering from anorexia nervosa—she comes from a white, upper-middle-class family that places heavy emphasis on high achievement, perfection, eating patterns, and physical appearance, and by refusing to eat she feels she has some control over her own life.[3]

This is a volatile study of family discord, and the drama of the story, though it sometimes seems exaggerated, clearly portrays the struggles of family and friends as well as those of Emily herself to find balance and control.

MEETING THE CHALLENGE

There are now far more books in which the main character is physically challenged in some way than there were even 10 years ago, but too few of them present the challenge in a convincing way.

Gregory Maguire's *Missing Sisters* (1994) features a protagonist who is partially deaf, has a speech defect, and because she has been raised in a convent, has had little experience dealing with others her own age. There is more to this story than the issue of deafness. Alice is not only hard of hearing; she is also an orphan who is losing all hope of being adopted, especially when on impulse, she turns down an apparently nice couple willing to take her because it doesn't feel right. It is up to Alice to meet the challenges that face her and come to an understanding of what she wants for herself.

SOCIAL ISSUES AND THE ADOLESCENT

In the early 1970s, the parents of a 15-year-old girl decided to publish her diary posthumously; the result was *Go Ask Alice* (1971), a narrative about the devastating effects of drug addiction. The book portrays the desperate need of an adolescent girl to communicate with her family and her failure to do so, leading to her death at an early age from a drug overdose.

The book generates controversy because many parents want to protect their children from reality. This is a stark portrait, its message unforgettable and highly disturbing. But throughout the story, all the signs of impending disaster are evident to those with the maturity to recognize them. *Go Ask Alice*, ideally, should be read by parents, then made part of a family discussion. Though parents would like to keep their children out of harm's way, young people are influenced by their peers and by the media; the longer a family pretends that life is an uncomplicated ideal, the harder it will be for a young person to go out in the world and make educated choices.

If this discussion attempted to include a book for each physical, emotional, or mental challenge that faces young people during adolescence, one chapter could expand into an entire book. The issues covered in this chapter barely touch the surface of the subjects examined in today's books for children and young adults, but the books under scrutiny here can lead to a better understanding of the factors that sometimes make it difficult to communicate with adolescents. The bibliography that follows includes several titles not discussed in this chapter, in an effort to expand the list of recommended issue-related books.

NOTES

1. Marilyn R. Singer, School Library Journal (December 1972), pp. 60–61.
2. Herbert N. Foerstel. *Banned in the U.S.A.: A Reference Guide to Book Censorship in Schools and Public Libraries.* Westport, Conn.: Greenwood, 1994, pp. 57, 123–124.
3. "Health Information for Patients: Facts about Anorexia Nervosa." American Academy of Family Physicians. Available on-line. URL: http://www.aafp.org/patientinfo/anorexia.html. Updated on July 22, 1998.

ANNOTATED BIBLIOGRAPHY

Anonymous. *Go Ask Alice.* Englewood Cliffs, N.J.: Prentice-Hall, 1971; New York: Aladdin, 1998. (Young Adult)

> This powerful narrative begins with ordinary events in the life of a 15-year-old girl who writes in her new diary: "Yesterday when [Roger] asked me out, I thought I would literally and completely die with happiness." But she goes on to say, when Roger cancels the date, ". . . now the whole world is cold and gray and unfeeling and my mother is nagging me to clean up my room." Within only a few pages of this diary, it becomes obvious that the writer, known as Alice in this text, suffers from low self-esteem, impending bulimia, and the seesaw emotions of adolescence. When she moves to a new community with her parents and is faced with all the new adjustments, it isn't surprising that she relishes a substance that seems to make all her problems disappear. She is unwittingly introduced to drugs in a drink at a party and finds herself in a state of euphoria. With drugs it becomes easier and easier to forget her problems, and her drug use accelerates. Before

long, however, it is evident that drugs are controlling her very existence, and this terrifying loss of control brings on depression. Because she is unable to communicate her fears to her parents, and because they don't recognize the signs, Alice is unable to overcome her addiction. This is a book that has not lost its impact in the years since it was published and would be useful in a discussion between parents and children about peer pressure and substance abuse.

Block, Francesca Lia. *Weetzie Bat.* New York: HarperCollins, 1989. (Young Adult)

Norma Klein and other authors writing in the early 1970s about formerly taboo subjects such as divorce, sex, death, and drugs were accused of sensationalism, of blatantly flaunting social mores, but by the time Block wrote *Weetzie Bat,* reviewers saw in the story a compelling but disturbing portrait of a young woman far more responsible than her parents. Weetzie's parents are separated, and she lives with two young men, her friends Dirk and Duck, who are gay. In a combination of stark realism and fantasy, Weetzie meets her Secret Agent Lover Man, lives with him, and has a child, Cherokee. She also accepts Witch Baby, Child of Secret Agent Lover Man and Vixanne Wigg, into the family. Witch Baby becomes the subject of Block's second book.

———. *Witch Baby.* New York: HarperCollins, 1991. (Young Adult)

The author of *Weetzie Bat* (1989) follows up with a story featuring Weetzie's daughter, Witch Baby, whose casual way of life in a "to-each-his-own" family has caused her to feel abandoned and unloved. Witch Baby finds herself searching for self-esteem and a sense of identity in an unorthodox Los Angeles society. She meets her real mother, Vixanne, finds out who her real father is, and returns to the fold, accepting her place in the family.

Byars, Betsy. *The Pinballs.* New York: Harper, 1977, 1993. (Middle Reading)

By the time Carlie is sent to a foster home because she and her stepfather can't get along, she has set up her own barriers and makes it clear to the other two foster children under Mrs. Mason's care that Carlie makes the rules. Gradually, as she, Harvey, and Thomas J. settle in with Mrs. Mason, Carlie begins to reach out and take a tentative chance on friendship with these two boys who, it turns out, need her as much as she needs them.

————. *The Summer of the Swans.* New York: Viking, 1970; New York: Puffin, 1996. NEWBERY MEDAL. (Middle Reading)

> Sara Godfrey finds her 14th summer to be a maelstrom of emotions. She never knows from one moment to the next how she's going to feel. She hates the way she looks and worries constantly about how she appears to others. Her sister, Wanda, is beautiful, and her younger brother, Charlie, as much as she adores him, hasn't spoken a word since he was three and needs watching over constantly. The summer of the swans is Sara's summer of discontent—until Charlie disappears, and Sara begins to understand what is truly important in her life.

Creech, Sharon. *Walk Two Moons.* New York: HarperCollins, 1994. NEWBERY MEDAL. (Young Adult)

> Although this novel at first appears to be an exploration of 13-year-old Salamanca Tree Hiddle's American Indian roots, it becomes a story about maturity: making choices, sorting things out, changing that which can be changed, and accepting that which cannot. Sal weaves her own story in and out of the story she tells her grandparents as they travel across the country to visit Sal's mother, who left one day and never came back.

Danziger, Paula. *The Pistachio Prescription.* New York: Dell, 1978, 1990. (Middle Reading)

> Cassie, at 13, is convinced that her family is the bane of her existence. When she and her mother go shopping for clothes, her mother adds extensively to her own wardrobe and Cassie chooses only what she really needs. Cassie knows that as soon as her father sees the bill, World War III will begin in the household. She decides it's much easier for her to live in a dreamworld. Besides, she has asthma, and facing reality—running for class president, dealing with her hyperactive family, accepting her own physical shortcomings—is much too difficult. Or is it?

Frank, Lucy. *I Am an Artichoke.* New York: Bantam Doubleday Dell, 1995. (Middle Reading)

> Sarah, age 15, takes a summer job as a mother's helper in New York City and discovers that it's not the mother but the daughter she is expected to help. Emily is only a few years younger than Sarah and resents Sarah's presence in the home.

Emily keeps to herself, but it soon becomes evident that she is anorexic, and her mother refuses to accept that anything is wrong. As Sarah begins to gain Emily's trust, the story becomes a sensitive exploration of an illness that is brought on by a lack of self-esteem and unrealistic expectations.

Garden, Nancy. *Annie on My Mind.* Reissue paperback. New York: Farrar, Straus, Giroux, 1982; New York: Harcourt Brace, 1992. (Young Adult)

This sensitive story of two teenage girls, Eliza and Annie, tackles the issue of homosexuality by exploring its emotional side. When Eliza meets Annie, she immediately has the feeling that Annie is her soul mate, but their relationship is threatened by the rigid social codes of Eliza's ultraconservative background. In her private school setting, her relationship with Annie is considered unacceptable by the school supervisor and her assistant, who make more of the situation than is warranted. This leads to a confrontation with school officials and with Eliza's parents that, through understanding and acceptance, ends in Eliza's favor.

Greene, Bette. *Them That Glitter and Them That Don't.* New York: Knopf, 1983. (Young Adult)

Carol Ann Delaney is the daughter of an Irish father and a Gypsy mother and, at 17, wants more than anything to succeed as a country and western singer. Her mother, on the other hand, looks into her crystal ball and predicts total failure for Carol Ann if she pursues her dream. Carol Ann, who has never been convinced of her mother's powers before, begins to question whether she should settle down with Will Bellows, who has asked her to marry him, and accept the security that Will offers on his successful dairy farm. Or should she believe in herself enough to actually go to Nashville and try to make it? Jean McCaffrey, Carol Ann's music teacher, believes in her, but Mrs. McCaffrey is a gorgio, a non-Gypsy, and Gypsies don't trust gorgios. Only Carol Ann can decide how to spend her life after high school graduation.

MacLachlan, Patricia. *The Facts and Fictions of Minna Pratt.* New York: HarperCollins, 1988, 1990. (Middle Reading)

MacLachlan brings her talent for characterization to this rite-of-passage story. Minna Pratt has trouble dealing with her peculiar family and with her own idiosyncrasies, but all of that fades when Lucas comes into her life. Minna's existence takes on new meaning, and her fears fade. Even so, Minna wishes she could communicate with her mother, a writer who is, according to Minna's father, in the "land of la." He likes her there; Minna doesn't. But when she writes to her mother as a fan, using an assumed name, and says, "My mother doesn't really hear what I say. She doesn't listen," she makes a startling discovery.

Maguire, Gregory. *Missing Sisters.* Dublin: O'Brien Press, 1994; New York: Hyperion, 1998. (Young Adult)

Alice isn't completely deaf, but her hearing loss and a speech impediment keep her isolated much of the time. She is being raised in a convent, having been abandoned as an infant 11 years earlier; the only sister she really feels close to, Sister Vincent de Paul, is burned in a fire at the convent, and Alice is more isolated than ever. Then, at summer camp, Alice is mistaken for a girl named Miami, who turns out to be her identical twin, except that Miami isn't deaf, has no speech defect, and has been adopted by a family. Alice dares to hope Miami's family will adopt her as well, but there are obstacles to such a happy ending, and Alice must decide what she really wants and how to attain it.

Ryden, Hope. *Wild Horse Summer.* Illus. Paul Casale. New York: Clarion, 1997. (Middle Reading)

When Alison, 13, travels to her uncle's ranch in Wyoming, she is apprehensive about meeting her blind cousin, Kelly. She is concerned that she will be expected to lead Kelly around and watch out for her. But Kelly is far more self-sufficient than Alison, and it is Kelly, with her "seeing-eye" horse, who watches out for Alison. When Kelly's horse, Cookie, is abducted by a wild stallion, Alison has the opportunity to forget her own fear of heights and horses to help rescue her cousin's horse.

Wersba, Barbara. *Tunes for a Small Harmonica.* New York: Harper, 1976. (Young Adult)

J. F. McAllister dresses like a boy, much to her mother's chagrin, and at age 15 becomes concerned she might be a suppressed homosexual. After reading everything she can find on the subject, she decides she is not. Instead, she falls in love with her poetry teacher, Harold Murth, who is much older than she. J. F. has never had to worry about finances; her family is well-to-do. She also has never set her mind to anything, but her commitment to loving Harold Murth creates a need for her to attain a specific goal for the first time in her life. J. F. makes several discoveries in a short time. She loves to play the harmonica and finds she is quite good at it. Her dream of spending her life with Harold Murth comes to an unexpected end. And her psychiatrist, Dr. Waingloss, is not the refuge she thought he would be—in fact, he begins to confide in her, much to her horror. This book, at the time it was written, was boldly unorthodox, but J. F., in the 1990s, is simply one of many young people just like her.

6

WHAT ARE LITTLE GIRLS MADE OF? DOUBTING SELF

Self-confidence is a real
thing, and its absence
devastates. Any critics who
believe self-esteem is
baloney, I invite them to
visit my high school kids.

—Susan,
Prodigy Books & Writing
Bulletin Board

During adolescence, something untoward happens. Pleasing one's peers suddenly becomes paramount, and the "junk values of mass culture,"[1] which stress impossible levels of beauty and romance, strip away the self-esteem and self-confidence that carried little girls blithely through childhood. These new, false values also lead girls to the books of mass culture—series books, romance novels, and sequel after sequel. Parents can't cancel adolescence for their daughters, but they can anticipate the problems and help make the transition easier by becoming aware of the content of such books and how they influence female identity. Some of the titles discussed in this chapter reflect attitudes now obsolete; others are more contemporary but still present an underlying prejudice. All require a second look. At first reading, plot tends to overshadow character, and the story's influence on identity may be overlooked. A careful look at characterization in these books, however, reveals hidden messages.

DEVELOPMENT OF GENDER ROLES

Adolescence is not the first time girls become aware of gender roles, of course. Many books for young readers, some published decades ago and still popular, introduce girls to traditional, often outdated, expectations. Children's books before the 1970s presented childhood as a time of innocence. Gender roles were clearly set forth, as in Inez Hogan's *The Upside Down Book* (1955), which presented "A Story for Little Boys" in pages of blue and "A Story for Little Girls" all in pink, with a teddy bear for the boy and a doll for the girl. Activities for the boy included climbing trees, sliding down hills, and dealing with accidental falls, while the girl takes her doll to the park and tells her to be careful, gets a Popsicle and warns the doll not to get it on her dress, and at the end of the day makes sure all her toys are put away. A child reading this book learns that boys are expected to be active and girls are expected to be passive. This assumption still exists, with parents of toddlers taking pride in the fact that their little boy is drawn to guns and trucks, while their little girl loves playing house. Whether this behavior is inborn or learned is still being debated.

In Carolyn Haywood's popular *"B" Is for Betsy* (1939), a story about five-year-old Betsy's kindergarten experiences, almost every stereotype defining gender is present. Betsy depends on Father to resolve any problem she faces; the teachers in Betsy's school are all females; the traffic monitor is a police*man;* all of the animals in the book are male, except for one dog, who has to be a female because she has puppies—male puppies. Pink is the prevalent color for girls: a pink-and-white tea set on a bed of pink cotton, pink roses and pink candles on Betsy's friend Ellen's birthday cake, even pink ice cream. At a costume party, Betsy is dressed in pink, while her friend Billy carries a whip and wears a toy revolver in his belt. In this book, grandmothers bake cookies and mothers are housewives.

In pre-1970s children's books, the transition from childhood to adolescence was rarely discussed. Happy endings were the rule, and subjects such as divorce, sex, drugs, and death were avoided. Haywood's books reflect the social climate of the 1930s and 1940s, when children were protected from adult concerns. The popularity of *"B" Is for Betsy* has continued, regardless of its stereotypes, because there were and still are few chapter books directed at five-year-olds. The larger print and simple language appeals to early readers.

When Maud Hart Lovelace wrote *Betsy-Tacy* (1940), she avoided stereotypes altogether and even managed to make a reference to the death of one character's baby sister. This is a story of two five-year-old girls who are independent and imaginative and develop a close friendship, solving their own problems instead of seeking adult intervention.

According to feminist theorist Judy Mann, imagination helps many girls through various forms of adversity as they grow up. One common fantasy of girlhood is to be descended from royal blood, which, when revealed, will allow a little girl to reign supreme "over her father and other grown men."[2] Frances Hodgson Burnett's *A Little Princess* (1905) is an example of this type of fantasy, although in the case of young Sara Crewe, she has always been a princess to her father. When he is reported dead, she loses her status and is abused by the schoolmistress and jealous classmates. Her status is eventually restored through the efforts of adult males, but Sara, through it all, retains her self-confidence and belief in herself and shares these qualities with the other girls at the school.

As a topic of class discussion in schools, the story can be seen as a reflection of the social class system in 19th-century England. Sara exhibits strength of character and the ability to empathize with others, traits that ultimately endear her to her peers, and good storytelling in this popular book eclipses any tendency toward didacticism.

NANCY DREW, SERIES PIONEER

While *A Little Princess* takes place in England, where class distinction prevails, the indomitable and independent Nancy Drew is the American version of royalty, a superstar who rises above the ordinary and becomes the personification of a dream for many little girls. Although she made her debut in 1930, she exhibits attributes that many young girls still admire today: She is clever, brave, and determined, yet stylish and graceful. She shows none of the ambiguities that typically beset girls in early adolescence. As author Karen Plunkett-Powell says of the Nancy Drew series as originally conceived, "[Nancy Drew] has star quality." She is the "Barbie of the written word, the Shirley Temple of the teen set, the Dorothy of detection, complete with her own Oz-like hometown of River Heights and her own dog named Togo."[3]

In early versions of the series, though Nancy may look down on those she considers inferior, she always solves her cases and never lets boy-girl feelings interfere with her goals. She works well alone or with others. When Edward Stratemeyer created her, and Mildred Wirt Benson (the first "Carolyn Keene") established her personality in *The Secret of the Old Clock* (1930), Nancy was already beyond adolescence and wasn't concerned about what others thought of her. Her enthusiasm was infectious as she set out to solve every case that came her way.

Unfortunately, when a new version of the series, called the "Nancy Drew Files," was created in the 1980s, the qualities that originally made Nancy a role model were submerged in an effort to make her one of the in-crowd, where she is more concerned with romance than mystery. These later books focus on plot rather than character, and Nancy seems to have a lesser role.

Nancy Drew, American princess personified, has always been the most popular female sleuth in the series genre, but she wasn't the only one to make an appearance in the 1930s. In 1932, the first Judy Bolton mystery (*The Haunted Attic*) was published, and that popular series continued until 1967. The 38 books in the 35-year series recently were reissued in facsimile editions and perhaps because all were conceived and written by the same author—Rachel Irene Beebe under the pseudonym Margaret Sutton—the character of Judy Bolton is more realistic than that of Nancy Drew. Judy is bright and compassionate, but she isn't perfect. She cares what people think of her. " 'I'm not afraid of anything,' [Judy] declare[s], 'unless—unless it's being unpopular. I want people to like me.' "[4] She also moves from one neighborhood to another and has to adjust to a new environment, while Nancy's hometown, River Heights, offers stability. For a time, Judy's worst fears come true when she is shunned by her schoolmates. Nancy Drew represents an idealized "James Bond" image, while Judy Bolton can be considered the forerunner to the characters in Judy Blume's realistic, issue-related books of the 1970s. At the time the Judy Bolton series was written, no other books for girls addressed the concerns of adolescence.

THE RISE OF JUDY BLUME

With the introduction of Margaret in Judy Blume's *Are You There, God? It's Me, Margaret* (1970), puberty became the pop subject of the day. Margaret Simon, at age 11, hasn't started her period yet and wants desperately to get her first bra. Her character speaks directly to generations of girls with these concerns, and Margaret's story is their story. Blume has used her ear for adolescent dialogue, male and female, in many books for children over the years. The title heroine of *Deenie* (1973), who discovers she has scoliosis and has to wear a brace, is devastated because her physical impairment sets her apart from her peers, and she's convinced they will reject her. *Blubber* (1974) is the story of Linda, who is overweight and persecuted by her peers, a victim of the often unrealistic expectations of a looks-obsessed culture.

Blume became so popular with girls on the verge of adolescence that when she wrote *Forever* (1975), intended for young adults, younger girls also read it. Since it is a story about a teenager's decision to have sex with her boyfriend, many parents and librarians became concerned about its effect on younger readers. But the romance in the book is tempered by Blume's step-by-step descriptions of the sexual process, with emphasis on birth control and protection against sexual diseases. The book continues to be popular with today's teenagers, and adults who read it can appreciate its value as a sex-education tool.

Judy Blume filled a void in literature for girls, and the general public has responded enthusiastically to her books, but Blume's books alone will not act as the sustaining force to help a girl through adolescence. Blume delves into different issues, but her resolutions are either unrealistic or avoided altogether. Variety is the key.

CONTEMPORARY SERIES

Books that features strong young women who have preserved their own identity transmit a much deeper message to girls than books in the popular Goosebumps and Fear Street series by R. L. Stine, which offer shallow characterizations and minor roles for females. Stine's Kat in *It Came from Beneath the Sink!* (Goosebumps, 1995) and Corky in *Cheerleaders: The New Evil* (Fear Street, 1994) lack the qualities that would make them role models for girls. And because these books are as apt to be read by girls as by boys, the lack of character exhibited by the females confirms a female adolescent's lack of self-esteem.

Stine has made the comment "that kids as well as adults are entitled to books of no socially redeeming value."[5] It's one thing to present stories that focus on action rather than character; it's quite another to present stories that not only label girls as almost totally dependent on boys but also present a cast of characters who show no remorse for wrongdoing. The overall attitude of the characters in Stine's books is, "Honestly, folks, it's not my fault." Parents might want to supplement these series with books that offer a more positive portrait of boys *and* girls. Chances are, the children themselves will start looking for more content in the books they read.

After reading a few Goosebumps and Fear Street books, the Baby-sitters Club series by Ann Martin is, at first, a welcome relief. It is, after all, a series in which girls have the leading roles. But a second look calls for further appraisal. While R. L. Stine prides himself on avoiding social redemption in his books, Martin's series offers interchangeable do-good characters who invariably learn at least one lesson, sometimes more. As in many series books, the characters are totally predictable. Each featured character reacts thoughtlessly to adversity, as in the Stine books, blaming someone else for her problems, but in contrast to the Stine books, Martin's characters finally realize the error of their ways. Even so, there is no spontaneity in these books, and although each member of the Baby-sitters Club is carefully assigned traits intended to set her apart from the rest, the girls are basically the same person, regardless of ethnic or social background.

Claudia, for example, is a Japanese-American member of the Baby-sitters Club, but in *Claudia and Crazy Peaches* (1994), any ethnic distinction that might exist within her family is ignored. Claudia, born an American, can't spell, eats lots of junk food, and has artistic talent. She is "a typical teenager," but Martin has overlooked the opportunity to show the cultural conflicts that sometimes occur within families when American values clash with the family's heritage.

Kristy is the president and founder of the Baby-sitters Club; in *Kristy and Mr. Mom* (1995), her family reflects contemporary America with sisters and brothers, stepsisters and stepbrothers, and even a four-year-old adopted sister from Vietnam. In the first book in the series, *Kristy's Great Idea* (1986), Kristy, whose mother is divorced and has to work outside the home, finds it difficult to juggle baby-sitting chores between family and neighborhood and has the idea to start a baby-sitters club with her friends. By the time of *Kristy and Mr. Mom*, Kristy's mother is married to a millionaire, who is also divorced with children, and the family has increased to 10 members, including Kristy's grandmother, who has taken on responsibility for domestic chores.

When Kristy's stepfather has a mild heart attack and decides to stop working and take over the running of the household, misunderstandings occur and chaos prevails until the family gets together and comes up with a solution. In this story, Kristy's mother has been relegated to the background, and it's not at all clear where she spends her days. Martin seems to be trying so hard to reflect a politically correct society, with a stepfather who shares household chores, a grandmother who is more active than passive, and a mother who is not limited to home and family, that the mother's role in the family is lost in the shuffle. The conflict occurs between Kristy's stepfather and her grandmother, with grandmother moving into her own apartment when it doesn't seem that she is needed any longer, then moving back when Kristy's stepfather admits he can't both run a household and handle increasing business duties. It's difficult to identify the role model in this book, if indeed there is one, unless it's the stepfather who finally accepts his own shortcomings and admits he can't do everything himself.

The American Girl Collection does a better job of differentiating between the various protagonists than the Baby-sitters Club series does, because each of the featured characters lives at a different time in American history. Every book, however, follows exactly the same format. The series was developed by the Pleasant Company, a small publisher in Wisconsin, and became so successful that it was picked up by Scholastic and widely distributed, with books, dolls, and accessories representing specific eras in American history. The books are written by and credited to a variety of authors, all of whom follow a preplanned story line that offers details of American society in the year assigned to each of six main characters: Felicity, Kirsten, Addy, Samantha, Molly and a new character, Josefina.

Samantha Learns a Lesson: A School Story (1986), by Susan S. Adler, is set in a small town called Mount Bedford in 1904. Samantha's world includes a wide gap between wealth and poverty, a continuing reliance on English mores, a prejudicial but growing education system, and many technological advances. At the end of the book, facts concerning the growth of the American education system in the early part of this century are presented with selected photographs from the period. Each book concludes with a similar summary of American history as it relates to the chosen theme, and the story line is deliberately educational. *Happy Birthday, Samantha! A Springtime Story* (1991) by Valerie Tripp includes a chapter about the efforts of Susan B. Anthony and other suffragists to gain voting rights for women. In this particular story, the focus on willingness to accept change takes over the story line, and Samantha is little more than an onlooker as those around her deal with the issues.

As a social studies supplement, the American Girl series presents history as experienced by the females of a particular era, offering a viewpoint that in past years has been ignored in history textbooks. As a guide to character development, however, the series falls short.

Series books have a tendency to lack character development because they are based on a recurring storyline that is predictable and unchanging. It is therefore not surprising that their popularity depends more on how soon the next book will come out than on how compelling the previous books might have been.

BEHIND THE POPULARITY

Parents, teachers, and librarians are quick to criticize the series book, while many books that have found a niche as a literary classic, such as *Mr. Popper's Penguins* (1938), enjoy continued popularity no matter how old-fashioned or outdated their messages might be. As entertainment, *Mr. Popper's Penguins,* written by Richard Atwater and revised by his wife, Florence Atwater,[6] appeals to middle-grade readers who appreciate its humor and the far-fetched adventures that result from having a penguin as a pet in a residential neighborhood. In a reflection of the time in which it was written, however, it portrays a less than positive view of female identity.

The Poppers live in a small city called Stillwater, and Mr. Popper is a house painter. He and his wife have two children, a girl and a boy, and like many in the Great Depression of the 1930s, the family struggles to get by, especially since Mr. Popper's job is seasonal. It is Mr. Popper's dream to go to the South Pole, but a letter to Admiral

Drake instead brings a penguin to his home in Stillwater, a penguin who gets lonesome and needs a mate, and pretty soon the Poppers have not 2 but 12 penguins.

Mrs. Popper lacks a distinct identity. She accepts every decision her husband makes and devotes her life to her family. While she does her mending, Mr. Popper reads travel books. She does the marketing and frequently has to clean up after her husband, children, and penguins, but she gets no help from her out-of-work husband.

Shallow characterizations of females in children's books do little to increase the prestige of women, and far too many popular children's books have a tendency to relegate girls to a lesser role. Such oversights increase the value of books that feature heroic females in roles that give them equal status and confirm their value in society.

Fortunately, children's books in general have reached a higher level of sophistication in the last decades of this century, and books that offer layers of meaning are more common today. With academics beginning to include children's literature in their studies, there is more demand for quality, for plain good writing, than on what lessons a children's book might teach. Early children's books that have lasted as originally written are those in which character development and artistic use of language create multiple levels of meaning, calling for further exploration of content.

NOTES

1. Mary Pipher. *Reviving Ophelia: Saving the Selves of Adolescent Girls.* New York: Ballantine Books, 1994, p. 23.
2. Judy Mann. *The Difference: Growing Up Female in America.* New York: Warner Books, 1994, pp. 266–267.
3. Karen Plunkett-Powell. *The Nancy Drew Scrapbook.* New York: St. Martin's Press, 1993, p. 6.
4. Margaret Sutton [Rachel Irene Beebe]. *The Haunted Attic.* Bedford, Mass.: Applewood Books, 1994, p. 43.
5. Anne Commire, ed. "R.L. Stine." *Something About the Author: Facts and Pictures about Authors and Illustrators of Books for Young People.* Vol. 31. Detroit: Gale Research, 1983, p. 160.
6. Bette J. Peltola. "Atwater, Richard; Atwater, Florence." In *Children's Books and Their Creators: An Invitation to the Feast of Twentieth-*

Century Children's Literature, edited by Anita Silvey. Boston: Houghton Mifflin, 1995, p. 35.

ANNOTATED BIBLIOGRAPHY

Adler, Susan S. *Samantha Learns a Lesson: A School Story.* New York: Scholastic, 1986. (Early Reading)

> In 1904, Samantha discovers that while she takes her own education for granted, other children are less fortunate and in fact are expected to spend long days working in factories. She takes on the job of teaching Nellie, a young factory worker, how to read and write after she helps Nellie find a less demanding position in a private home. Samantha ignores the jibes of her private-school classmates, who look down on her young friend.

Atwater, Richard, and Florence Atwater. *Mr. Popper's Penguins.* Illus. Robert Lawson. Boston: Little, Brown, 1938, 1992. (Middle Reading)

> This popular novel, originally published in 1938, focuses on Mr. Popper and his penguins; Mrs. Popper and their two children are relegated to lesser roles. Mr. Popper takes it for granted that his family will go along with his obsession with penguins, even when his penguin stable multiplies from 1 to 2 to 12 and the whole family has to travel across the country with the penguins to earn money for the animals' upkeep. At the end of the book, Mr. Popper goes to Antarctica with his penguins, and Mom and the kids are left behind.

Blume, Judy. *Are You There, God? It's Me, Margaret.* New York: Bradbury, 1970; New York: Laurel Leaf, 1991. (Middle Reading)

> Eleven-year-old Margaret Simon is on the threshold of puberty. Her concerns about fitting in with her peers begin to accelerate when it seems that every girl except her wears a bra, has had her first period, and has to wear deodorant. Margaret's adjustment problems vacillate between her body and her spiritual identity as she tries to decide whether she wants to be Jewish like her father or Christian like her mother.

———. *Deenie.* New York: Bradbury, 1973; New York: Laurel Leaf, 1991. (Middle Reading)

> Deenie Fenner, at age 13, is pretty and vivacious. She has a good chance to make the cheerleading squad, but for some reason, she doesn't. When her mother takes her to a modeling agency for a tryout, she's rejected there as well. Deenie is very uncomfortable around physically imperfect people like Old

Lady Murray, who has a hump on her back, and Gena Courtney, a young neighbor who has braces on her legs and is blind in one eye. When Deenie discovers that she too has a defect, scoliosis, and has to wear a back brace for four years, she's convinced she'll never survive such an ordeal. At a time in her life when fitting in is the most important thing in her life, she's set apart—different!

Burnett, Frances Hodgson. *A Little Princess.* Philadelphia: Lippincott, 1905; New York: Dell Yearling, 1975. (Middle Reading)

When Sara Crewe's wealthy father leaves her in the care of Miss Minchin at a private English school while he returns to India, Sara enjoys her princesslike status. But when her father disappears and is declared a pauper, Miss Minchin's true nature comes through, and Sara quickly loses her elevated status, learning how to survive at the bottom of the social ladder. Her strength of character allows her to survive all kinds of adversity in this 1905 novel.

Haywood, Carolyn. *"B" Is for Betsy.* San Diego: Harcourt Brace, 1939, 1990. (Early Reading)

Betsy is five years old and just starting kindergarten. Although at first she doesn't want to go to school at all, she quickly makes friends and discovers that school is fun. In fact, she is first in her class at the end of the school year. Haywood has created a somewhat ideal character in Betsy, who has only one bad day in an entire year. She represents a parent's dream child, a prototype that little girls find impossible to emulate. Betsy is the subject of several more books in this series.

Keene, Carolyn [Stratemeyer Syndicate]. *The Secret of the Old Clock.* New York: Grosset and Dunlap, 1930; Bedford, Mass.: Applewood, 1991. (Middle Reading)

This is the first book of the long line of Nancy Drew mysteries, which follow a pattern so familiar that the entire series can be summed up with the following: Nancy Drew is faced with a mystery that only she is able to solve. She perseveres, even though she is warned to get off the case; both she and an innocent victim encounter villains and are imprisoned for a time. Nancy manages to escape, with the help of a "proper" male authority, then faces a crescendo of swift events that lead to her quickly solving the case. Nancy has been a role model to generations of young girls. It is worth noting, however, the villains in the series are almost invariably dark-skinned, poor, and uneducated. In early books they were Italian or Jewish; these days, they hail from the Middle East.

Martin, Ann M. *Claudia and Crazy Peaches* (The Baby-sitters Club #78). New York: Scholastic, 1991. (Middle Reading)

Claudia Kishi is ecstatic when she discovers that her favorite aunt, Peaches, is going to have a baby. But problems arise when Peaches and her husband, who are waiting for their new house to be built, temporarily move into the Kishi home. Aunt Peaches, who is impulsive and fun, keeps talking Claudia into leaving her homework to go off on different adventures. At first, Claudia is easily swayed, but she finally loses patience with her aunt and says things she regrets, especially when Peaches has a miscarriage and Claudia thinks it's her fault. A secondary story concerned with a baby-sitting dilemma runs through the book, involving all the baby-sitters in the club and alternating with Claudia's story. In this predictable series, all's well that ends well.

———. *Karen's Goldfish* (Baby-sitters Little Sister #16). New York: Scholastic, 1991. (Early Reading)

The easy-to-read Little Sister series is directed at girls in early elementary grades. The books introduce a dilemma on a much simpler level than that of the Baby-sitters Club series. In this book, Karen, stepsister of Kristy, feels left out because she doesn't have a pet of her own. Her father solves the problem by purchasing two goldfish, one for her and one for her brother, Andrew. Since Karen and her brother live with their mother and spend every other week with their father, Karen has to leave the care of the goldfish to her stepbrother, David Michael, when she's not there. She doesn't really trust him to do the job, and when her fish dies, she accuses David Michael of killing it. Her unreasonable accusation causes more problems for her than for David Michael, but eventually all misunderstandings are resolved and Karen gets a new fish.

———. *Karen's Worst Day* (Baby-sitters Little Sister #3). New York: Scholastic, 1989. (Early Reading)

In this early Little Sister book, Karen (see previous entry) becomes more discouraged as her day progresses, and nothing goes right. But eventually things take a turn for the better, and Karen is convinced the next day surely will be one of her best days.

———. *Kristy and Mr. Mom* (The Baby-sitters Club #81). New York: Scholastic, 1995. (Middle Reading)

When Kristy's stepfather, Watson Brewer, has a mild heart attack, he decides to stay at home and take care of the house. Things work out well until he and Kristy's grandmother, Nanny, clash when planning two different dinners. The two come to an agreement, but Nanny doesn't feel needed any more and moves into her own apartment. Then Watson's two children, Karen and Andrew, are due to spend the month with him, increasing the family to 10. As Watson gradually increases his office work at home, organization breaks down and suddenly the household is chaotic. Nanny is more needed than anyone realizes, and when Kristy and the rest of the family tell her so, she returns to share the load. In the meantime, the Baby-sitters Club is faced with a dilemma brought about by not making sure their clients know the club rules, and they finally come up with a solution.

Stine, R. L. *Cheerleaders: The New Evil* (Fear Street). New York: Pocket Books, 1994. (Middle Reading)

When something called "the evil" once again invades the cheerleading squad, people start dying horrible deaths, and Corky feels it is her responsibility to contain the threat because she is convinced she is the one who released it in the first place.

———. *It Came from Beneath the Sink!* (Goosebumps). New York: Scholastic, 1995. (Early Reading)

When Kat and Daniel discover a living, breathing spongelike creature under the kitchen sink, they name it Grool and look forward to showing it off. It soon becomes evident that the creature thrives on bad feelings and pain. When accidents happen and people are hurt, the children decide to get rid of Grool, only to discover that there doesn't seem to be any way to destroy it.

———. *Stay Out of the Basement* (Goosebumps). New York: Scholastic, 1995. (Early Reading)

Margaret's dad is an out-of-work botanist who spends inordinate amounts of time in the basement and makes it clear to Margaret and her brother, Casey, that he doesn't want them to go down there. But when they see their father eating plant food and when his actions become more bizarre, the two children decide that they have to find out what is going on, and they can do this only if they go to the basement.

Sutton, Margaret [Rachel Irene Beebe]. *The Haunted Attic.* New York: Grosset & Dunlap, 1932; Bedford, Mass.: Applewood Books, 1994. (Middle Reading)

Judy Bolton represents young people of yesterday and today in a mystery interspersed with issues that all adolescent girls face. She wants to be liked and accepted, and she's afraid the boy she likes prefers someone else. When Judy moves into a new neighborhood with her family, she discovers that the house borders a wealthy section of town on one side and the beginning of a poorer section on the other. In addition to searching for clues to explain mysterious happenings in the new house, Judy is faced with a social boycott by the students at Girls' High when she makes friends with the girls who work in the mills. With the help of her resourceful brother, Horace, Judy proves her mettle by solving a longtime mystery and making the right choices in her social life.

Tripp, Valerie. *Happy Birthday, Samantha! A Springtime Story.* New York: Scholastic, 1991. (Early Reading)

This American Girl story is set in 1904 and in one chapter, focuses on women's struggle for the right to vote. Samantha and her Grandmary travel to New York City to visit Aunt Cornelia and Uncle Gard. Samantha gets lost on an outing and ends up at the park where Cornelia is making a suffragist speech at a feminist rally. Samantha is concerned that her grandmother, who believes women should know their place, will be angry. But she underestimates Grandmary's ability to compromise when human rights are at stake, even though her grandmother still feels that the old ways are best.

7

MISTRESS MARY, QUITE CONTRARY: CHALLENGING SELF

Until recently, adolescent girls haven't been studied by academics, and they have long baffled therapists.

—Mary Pipher, *Reviving Ophelia: Saving the Selves of Adolescent Girls*

Any books for young people that meet conflict head on are apt to raise questions as to their suitability for young readers. Judy Blume's *Deenie* (1973) (see pages 108–109), as well as *The Great Gilly Hopkins* (1978) by Katherine Paterson, for example, have been removed from some school libraries simply because of a brief reference in the first to masturbation and because the second contains "swear words."[1] Perhaps the real concern for some people, for those who practice censorship, is that these books address very real traumas that adolescents are likely to face—physical imperfection in *Deenie* (the main character has scoliosis) and in *Gilly Hopkins* abandonment, subjects that were avoided in children's books until the 1970s. Female protagonists in books written in the first part of the 20th century for the most part exhibited characteristics that were considered acceptable for young women, and if the characters were initially rebellious, they eventually followed the path of least resistance by demonstrating proper behavior well before the end of the book. The controversy in these books has more to do with the characters in the stories than with public criticism of content.

EMOTIONAL TRAUMA

Mary Lennox in *The Secret Garden* (1911), by Frances Hodgson Burnett, is thoroughly disagreeable at the start of the book, but when her parents die and she is sent from India to England, she finds herself part of a caring environment. This change results not only in a turnabout in her attitude toward others; it also allows her to help transform her cousin Colin from a social misfit into a self-sufficient and active young man. Any young person who has been made to feel alone and unloved can relate to Mary and dream of a similar resolution in his or her own life.

Anne Shirley in *Anne of Green Gables* (1908) (see page 67) is also an orphan who has never known love, but she quickly endears herself to Matthew and Marilla, who have taken her in. Anne quite easily adapts to her new life and to the ministrations of a caring couple.

Quite different from the happy endings of these earlier books is the outcome for Harriet in Louise Fitzhugh's *Harriet the Spy* (1964), one of the earliest books to challenge children's book taboos.[2]

Louise Fitzhugh's Harriet the Spy *(1964) challenged children's book taboos with an unconventional main character.*

Fitzhugh created a mother and father who cannot relate to each other or to their only daughter, who is left to her own devices. Although Harriet is not an orphan, her parents take little interest in her and in fact, turn her care over to the nanny Harriet calls "Ole Golly." The conflicts that confront Harriet confuse and upset her, and Ole Golly, who truly cares for her young charge, does the best she can to offer advice.

Harriet takes Ole Golly's presence for granted until her parents, upset that Ole Golly and her gentleman friend have taken Harriet out to a late movie, dismiss her. Even though Ole Golly is reinstated the next day, Harriet realizes during her brief absence how much she depends on her. When Ole Golly does leave for good to get married, Harriet is abandoned once more. She is shunned at school when her classmates find her notebook containing observations about them, and Harriet must decide whether to stand by her convictions or compromise her honesty in order to be accepted by her peers.

Unlike most resolutions in children's books up until the 1960s, the author doesn't tie up all the loose ends to create a happy ending. Harriet receives valuable advice in a letter from Ole Golly just when she needs it most. She apologizes to those who feel betrayed by her in order to regain acceptance and win back her friends, but she never really changes her outlook.

Before *Harriet,* the characters in most children's books had adult role models whom they could and eventually did emulate. The traits exhibited by these adults offer guidelines for young people that might seem idealistic today, but a solid background in reading gives young people the experience they need to understand less conventional books like *Harriet the Spy,* in which Ole Golly is very wise and Harriet's parents are not.

Like Harriet, Claudia Kinkaid, in E. L. Konigsburg's *From the Mixed-Up Files of Mrs. Basil E. Frankweiler* (1967), is a contrary girl who characterizes the bid for personal independence that marked the 1960s in America. Claudia's self-reliance impresses wealthy Mrs. Frankweiler, who decides to make the 11-year-old her heir after observing her for an extended period of time. During this observation period, Claudia, with her brother Jamie, runs away from home and takes up residence at the Metropolitan Museum of Art. When she inadvertently manages to solve a long-standing mystery at the museum, Mrs. Frankweiler decides it's time for them to meet. Both Mrs. Frankweiler and Claudia qualify as role models that young girls can appreciate. Claudia might be unconventional and spontaneous in her sometimes misguided actions, but she shows that she learns from her mistakes. Mrs. Frankweiler shows her willingness to look beyond the obvious and recognize Claudia's worth.

The novel I remember having the greatest impact on me was *The Scarlet Letter*. From then on my life changed dramatically. I don't know how to explain that, but I can say I remember being very angry.

—Jo, Prodigy Books & Writing Bulletin Board

AN ANGRY SOCIETY

When Katherine Paterson wrote *The Great Gilly Hopkins* in 1978, she anticipated the serious social problems of unloved and abandoned children. When a child is abandoned by either parent, or at least *feels* abandoned, the result is invariably volatile anger. Gilly Hopkins is a reflection of contemporary problems in schools, with children, male and female, acting out, expressing deep anger, and causing disruptions in their classrooms. Gilly has been abandoned by her mother and goes from one foster home to the next until she meets Maime Trotter, a foster parent who honestly cares.

Gilly sees herself as superior to the people she manipulates, while the reader sees below the surface to the angry, desperate child crying out for someone to care. Gilly is confident that most people are stupid; everything she does is calculated to test authority, and she thrives on the adversity she creates. In this setting Gilly has the upper hand, but when she is put into a situation where there are no opposing forces, when honesty and lack of guile prevail, she doesn't know what to do. In Maime Trotter's care her defenses are threatened, and the only way she can think of to deal with this unexpected situation is to run away. But to do so, she needs money. When she finds a stash of money in the bookcase of Trotter's blind neighbor, Mr. Randolph, she takes it without a qualm. Then she discovers the balance of the money she needs for bus fare to California, where her mother lives, in Trotter's open purse and steals that as well. But Gilly doesn't make it to California; she stays on with Trotter and William Ernest, another foster child, until the day her grandmother shows up to take her "home" where her mother is scheduled to visit her. Instead of a conventional happy ending, the book concludes with a compromise on Gilly's part to accept what life offers and make the best of it.

In *Children's Literature Review,* one critic complains that *Gilly Hopkins* covers too many of society's ills—"racism, sexism, ageism, I.Q.ism, and just about all the other prejudices of our society."[3] But the biggest controversy over the book did not involve its story at all. As discussed in Herbert Foerstel's *Banned in the U.S.A.: A Reference Guide to Book Censorship in Schools and Public Libraries* (1994), it was attacked by the so-called Moral Majority; one educator condemned the book for its bad language—counting and listing 50 profane words, with page numbers—and another protested what she called "profanity, blasphemy, obscenities and derogatory remarks toward God."[4] This reaction would delight Gilly Hopkins, who takes the greatest pleasure in upsetting adults with "bad" language and other superficial concerns.

Katherine Paterson, child of missionaries and a missionary herself, was awarded the 1980 National Book Award and the 1977 Christopher Medal for novels, including *Gilly Hopkins,* that represent the "highest human spiritual values." Some of the people who complained about the book admitted that they had never read it.

DEFINING GENDER

Pippi Longstocking, the hero of Astrid Lindgren's book of the same name, became a role model for many American children in the 1950s when it was translated from the Swedish. The freedom Pippi enjoyed was unheard of in the United States. Children found her attractive (and parents were threatened by her) because Pippi had no family but managed to run her household on her own. Although Pippi is the female equivalent of a Paul Bunyan or Robinson Crusoe—bigger than life and as resourceful as they come—she is also a child.

Pippi's influence on girls in America has been deep and long lasting. Critic Kik Reeder sees Pippi as less than ideal for girls to emulate: "It is soon apparent," she says, "that Pippi isn't a girl at all, even a tomboy, but a boy in disguise. Astrid Lindgren has simply equipped Pippi with all the traits we have come to think of as male . . . white, male values; strength, wealth, success, defiance, and staunch unemotionalism."[5] But isn't this the very problem today's young women are trying to overcome? Why can't women share some of the traits long considered male, and why can't men share some of the traits labeled female?

NOTES

1. Herbert N. Foerstel. *Banned in the U.S.A.: A Reference Guide to Book Censorship in Schools and Public Libraries.* Westport, Conn.: Greenwood, 1994, pp. 57, 123–124.
2. Typical taboo subjects in children's books prior to the 1960s were death, birth, religion, sex, divorce, drugs, and family dissension.
3. Ellen R. Davidson. Review of *The Great Gilly Hopkins,* by Katherine Paterson. In *Children's Literature Review: Excerpts from Reviews, Criticism, and Commentary on Books for Children.* Vol. 7. Gerard J. Senick, ed. Detroit, Mich.: Gale Research, 1984, p. 236.
4. Foerstel, pp. 198–199.
5. Kik Reeder. "Pippi Longstocking—Feminist or Anti-Feminist." In *Children's Literature Review: Excerpts from Reviews, Criticism, and Commentary on Books for Children.* Vol. 1. Ann Block and Carolyn Riley, eds. Detroit, Mich.: Gale Research, 1976, p. 139.

ANNOTATED BIBLIOGRAPHY

Burnett, Frances Hodgson. *The Secret Garden*. Philadelphia: Lippincott, 1911; New York: Random House, 1993. (Middle Reading)

> Mary Lennox, the protagonist of this longtime favorite story, does not fit the role model category, at least not when the book begins. Up until the year this book was published, females in children's books generally were attractive in appearance and attitude, and any adversity they faced was not their fault. In *The Secret Garden*, however, Mary, the only child of parents who would prefer she didn't exist in the first place, looks and acts disagreeable, and she alienates everyone around her. But her life undergoes a drastic change when, at the age of 9, her parents and everyone she knows dies in a cholera epidemic: Mary is sent from India to live with an uncle in England. From an atmosphere in which her every whim was indulged, Mary finds herself with people who expect her to fend for herself. Gradually, because these people actually care about her, she blossoms into a self-reliant person who begins to give of herself to others. The neglected garden she discovers and brings back to life becomes a metaphor for herself.

Fitzhugh, Louise. *Harriet the Spy*. New York: Harper, 1964, 1990. (Middle Reading)

> Harriet Welsch, age 11, is a storyteller. Her imagination is so active that her daily observations, recorded in her notebook, go beyond truth and become embellished with high degrees of drama and description. She adds details about people that they might not want to see in print. Harriet is also an only child, whose parents don't include her in their lives. She puts loneliness aside and lives in her imagination until things start to go wrong and reality intrudes. First, the only person who seems to really care about her, her nanny Ole Golly, is temporarily dismissed by her parents, then leaves for good to get married. When Harriet's notebook, with her disconcertingly honest observations, is found by one of her classmates, the result is a school boycott against Harriet, compounding her loneliness. Even her best friend, Sport, turns against her when he hears what she has written about him. The question becomes, Has Harriet gained enough guidance from Ole Golly in her short life to deal with the problems facing her? And will the decisions she makes offer guidelines for those reading this book?

Klein, Norma. *Mom, the Wolf Man and Me.* New York: Pantheon, 1972. (Middle Reading)

> Eleven-year-old Brett, whose mother has never been married, finds it difficult to explain to her friends that she likes her family life the way it is. Her friends have difficulty understanding that childbirth and marriage are not necessarily connected. Brett and her mother have settled into a routine that suits them both, but her mother now has a serious boyfriend. Brett calls him the "Wolf Man," and resents that he is sleeping with her mother. The final blow comes when her mother decides to marry the Wolf Man, and Brett must learn to adapt to a family that now includes mother, father, and child.

Konigsburg, E. L. *From the Mixed-Up Files of Mrs. Basil E. Frankweiler.* New York: Atheneum, 1967; New York: Buccaneer Books, 1992. NEWBERY MEDAL. (Middle Reading)

> Wealthy dowager Mrs. Basil E. Frankweiler begins this book by telling the story of 11-year-old Claudia Kincaid, whom she has decided to make her heir. The viewpoint shifts to Claudia just as she is making a decision to run away from home and take up residence in the Metropolitan Museum of Art. She has been considering this move for some time and has made her plans carefully. She invites her brother Jamie to join her because he always has money. At first, the adventure meets her expectations and the two children enjoy avoiding discovery, but after a few days, the excitement wears off. Then Claudia unearths an old mystery and solves it. Mrs. Frankweiler is the key to the mystery at the museum. The statue that intrigues Claudia used to belong to her. Claudia and her brother are invited to meet Mrs. Frankweiler, whose lawyer, Saxonberg, happens to be Claudia and Jamie's grandfather.

Lindgren, Astrid. *Pippi Longstocking.* Trans. Florence Lamborn. New York: Viking, 1950; New York: Puffin, 1988. *Pippi Goes on Board.* Trans. Florence Lamborn. New York: Viking, 1957; New York: Puffin, 1977. *Pippi in the South Seas.* Trans. Gerry Bothmer. New York: Viking, 1959; New York: Puffin, 1977. (Early Reading)

> Pippi is what most young girls would like to be, a free spirit who not only has no adult supervision but also has a supply of gold coins that allows her to be independent. Her two young neighbors, Annika and Tommy, are more conventional and enjoy living vicariously through Pippi. For all her bravado, however, Pippi misses her father, who is said to be lost at sea, and regrets not having a mother, who died when she was a

baby. Pippi not only takes care of herself but also convinces the authorities that she can manage on her own. Tommy and Annika join Pippi in her adventures and bask in the glow of her independence. Pippi is exceptionally strong (she can lift her horse and carry him around), she is wealthy, and she is fearless (in *Pippi Goes on Board* she becomes so involved in watching a play that she rushes on stage to attack the villain). Pippi's lack of restraint in everything she does makes for entertaining adventures.

Paterson, Katherine. *The Great Gilly Hopkins.* New York: Crowell, 1978. (Middle Reading)

Galadriel Hopkins, 11, called Gilly, can't seem to fit in anywhere. She's been in three foster homes in less than three years. She likes to be in charge, and when she is taken to the home of Maime Trotter, she sets out to let Maime know that she's going to call the shots. But Maime seems impervious to Gilly's manipulative actions and just keeps on accepting her, no matter what. Gilly also has trouble figuring out her sixth grade teacher, Miss Harris, who never reacts the way Gilly thinks she should. When she finds herself unable to control the adults in her present situation, Gilly turns to a classmate, Agnes Stokes, who is even more needy than Gilly, and to William Ernest, another of Maime's foster children, for help in returning to her mother in California. Gilly will do whatever she must to achieve her goal, even break the law.

8

GREAT EXPECTATIONS: RESHAPING SELF

Books are the carriers of
civilization. Without books,
history is silent, literature
dumb, science crippled,
thought and speculation at a
standstill.

– Barbara Tuchman,
historian

A child's favorite books are often
consciously the models for, or the
most important influence on, his or
her later beliefs and ways of living.

—Jonathan Cott, *Pipers at the Gates of Dawn*

At no time in literary history have children's books been as important to a child's upbringing as they are now. This final chapter focuses on the most current children's books, especially those that present innovative, sometimes controversial, ideas. Choosing the most relevant titles of this decade is close to impossible, with at least 50,000 children's books or more published in the last 10 years.

In the late 1990s, on the verge of a new millennium, books compete with other media for a young person's time and attention, and young people are exposed to challenges and problems that children of previous generations did not have to face. There was a time when the "family hour" on television presented shows meant to be viewed by young people—comedy, variety, and "happy family" sitcoms, idealistic programs that may not have considered the stark reality of social problems, but allowed children to enjoy their childhood much longer than is the case today. Boundaries for acceptable behavior were more rigidly defined, at home and in the schools, and children were less likely to venture outside these boundaries.

Now, most sitcoms are about unmarried people having sex whenever the mood strikes them. News programs compete to present the most horrendous views of real-life tragedies. Problems that were once common only among adults have trickled down to children as young as seven or eight—drug abuse, smoking and drinking, assault and battery, even murder. The nuclear family has expanded to include stepfathers and stepmothers, stepsisters and stepbrothers, and the single parent has become more common.

SHARING INFORMATION AND ENTERTAINMENT

Just as good books offset bad books, good television programming offsets bad television programming. Channel choices are wide and varied, and parents who are aware of what their children are watching can generate discussions and suggest alternatives, just as they can do with books when they are familiar with their children's reading material.

> If a child is to keep alive his inborn sense of wonder, he needs the companionship of at least one adult who can share it, rediscovering with him the joy, excitement and mystery of the world we live in.
>
> —Rachel Carson, *The Sense of Wonder*

Should a children's book offer only examples of so-called acceptable role models for young people, as William Bennett makes an effort to do in *The Children's Book of Virtues* (1995)? Or is it just as important to present a character who exhibits traits that generate discussion and debate? Bennett's intentions are good at a time when a breakdown of moral integrity is widespread: He offers ethical examples in well-known stories for children. But the majority of role models he has chosen are male, and the few stories in his collection that include females don't allow them to portray any degree of independence. When there is a female protagonist, as in "There Was a Little Girl," the child is scolded for being too active. Bennett's comment about this poem is "We see what happens to us sometimes when we do not behave!" But according to the poem, if the little girl had been a little boy, there would have been no need for a scolding:

> Her mother heard the noise,
> And she thought it was the boys
> A-playing at a combat in the attic;
> But when she climbed the stair,
> And found Jemima there,
> She took and she did scold her, most emphatic.

The differences between male and female and how to honestly define those differences has long been a bone of contention.

Hearing a parent describe a daughter as feminine because she would rather play house than football and a boy as masculine because he likes to rough-house brings up the question Are these actual gender traits, or are they the result of social influence? How early are social influences imprinted on children? Certainly, girls and boys are physically different; the differences increase as children grow older and become all-consuming for adolescents. Books offer a direct connection to whatever problems young people are facing, helping them to feel less alone.

THE GROWING YEARS

In Gina Willner-Pardo's *Daphne Eloise Slater, Who's Tall for Her Age* (1997), the theme is a developing friendship between eight-year-old Daphne and her classmate Leonard DiMaggio. Leonard usually calls attention to the fact that Daphne is not only taller than he is, but also taller than anyone else in her class. But when Daphne and Leonard are paired in science class and are expected to work together dissecting a lamb's eyeball, he confides in her, and she sees a side of him that she had never before considered. Even though she promises she won't betray him, he continues to tease her, and she is tempted to tell. But a promise is a promise, and she slowly becomes aware that her feelings toward Leonard have softened; his teasing has lost its sting.

The format of this particular book appeals to younger readers, who are sometimes daunted by longer middle-grade fiction. There are only 48 pages in this chapter book, and every double-page spread has an illustration. The theme of sudden growth at an early age is one that often applies to girls and causes them to feel that they are the focus of ridicule or that they are physically unattractive.

The reality of a young girl who is too tall too soon and her method of dealing with a changing physical identity gives way to a multilevel quasi-fantasy for young adults in Patrice Kindl's *The Woman in the Wall* (1997). Anna at age seven is so painfully shy that she retreats into the walls of her house, cutting herself off from any kind of social interaction and using her carpentry skills to build herself a world inside the walls. A visit from the school psychologist

"It was hard to believe that this was the same kid who was always making fun of Daphne and calling her names." Daphne confronts a classmate in Daphne Eloise Slater, Who's Tall for Her Age *(1997) by Gina Willner-Pardo.*

takes her more deeply into herself. She lives inside the walls for seven years, and her family almost stops thinking about her, compounding her own perceived lack of substance. Anna never completely detaches from reality, but her actions are a metaphor for ensuing adolescent agony—her sense of identity is very nearly erased until her physical self betrays her by going through puberty, and she must adjust to a new identity.

Recent novels for young readers, such as Gregory Maguire's *Seven Spiders Spinning* (1994), develop female characters that exhibit independence and sensitivity, and Maguire gives them high self-esteem. In *Seven Spiders* Thekla Mustard, president of the girls' club Tattletales, says, "A cat is superior to a dog. A dog is superior to a cat. A girl is superior to a boy." Thekla has an answer for everything. Admitting that their club name was originally an insult coined by the boys, Thekla announces, "*We* own the language, and we transform it! Does the word *tattletales* suggest a clot of simpering namby-pambies, idiotic goody-goody two-shoes, authority bound *mushbrains?*" The rest of the girls respond, "NO!" When Miss Earth, an adored elementary school teacher, is threatened, the girls forget their determination to beat the boys, the boys set aside their vendetta against the girls, and the two groups work together to save Miss Earth's life when she is bitten by a poisonous spider. This is a book that equalizes the roles of male and female, and the story appeals to middle and upper elementary students of both sexes.

From Alice (*Alice's Adventures in Wonderland*) to Nancy (*Nancy Drew* mysteries) to Weetzie (*Weetzie Bat*), myriad girls in literature have exhibited confidence and belief in themselves. At the end of the century, new heroes and role models for all children are emerging as authors and illustrators try to define gender in a way that offers balance and understanding between men and women.

ANNOTATED BIBLIOGRAPHY

Babbitt, Lucy Cullyford. *Where the Truth Lies.* New York: Orchard Books, 1993. (Young Adult)
   Kyra has always been protected by the walls of Sanctuary, where reality takes precedence and science rules. When she is

chosen to travel to a cave that her father is convinced will prove the nonexistence of a higher power, she is joined by the Triber Eli and the Godslander Lillen, both of whom are equally convinced that his or her beliefs will be dominant when they enter the cave. Eli believes in many gods, and Lillen believes in one. Babbitt manages to tackle the issue of religious conflicts in a story for young adults with an ending that is satisfying and convincing.

Bennett, William J., ed. *The Children's Book of Virtues.* Illus. Michael Hague. New York: Simon & Schuster, 1995. (Early Reading)

As a compendium of stories that provide strong role models for girls, this book falls short, but the stories included are well known to parents—selections from Aesop, Robert Frost, mythology, folklore, and nursery rhymes, chosen to portray the essentials of good character.

Kindl, Patrice. *The Woman in the Wall.* Boston: Houghton Mifflin, 1997. (Young Adult)

Anna describes herself as "small and thin, with a face like a glass of water." She is the middle child in her family and as such feels that she lacks identity. When she retreats into the walls of her home, she's not surprised to discover that her family almost forget she exists. In a story that incorporates elements of fantasy, Anna hides in the walls of her Victorian house from the age of 7 to the age of 14 and finds herself facing puberty all alone. Her body, which she thought she controlled, betrays her by taking on substance, and Anna is forced to confront her own reality.

Konigsburg, E. L. *The View from Saturday.* New York: Atheneum, 1996. NEWBERY MEDAL. (Young Adult)

This is the story of four 12-year-olds who form a club and agree to meet each Saturday morning for tea. Konigsburg develops the plot with a narrative from each of the participants—Julian, Nadia, Ethan, and Noah—leading to how they managed to beat their schoolmates first in the seventh grade and then in the eighth grade in the Epiphany Middle School quiz bowl and make it all the way to the state finals. In the telling, the importance of individuality and connectedness become part of the story, as each of the central characters comes to terms with his or her personal identity.

Kovacs, Deborah, and James Preller. *Meet the Authors and Illustrators: 60 Creators of Favorite Children's Books Talk About Their Work.* New York: Scholastic, 1991. (Young Adult)

Profiling an equal number of men and women in the children's book industry, Kovacs and Preller offer unusual tidbits of information and a discussion by various authors and illustrators on their work habits and their feelings about their work. Each profile is two pages long and includes a photograph. Readers learn that storyteller Ashley Bryan was brought up in the Bronx and loves the sound of words; sometimes illustrator Trina Schart Hyman gets so frustrated at her drawing table she just has to cry, but even so, she keeps on working; the late Louise Fitzhugh based the character of Harriet in *Harriet the Spy* in part on her own childhood.

Maguire, Gregory. *Seven Spiders Spinning*. Illus. Dirk Zimmer. New York: Clarion Books, 1994. (Middle Reading)

On the way to a research center at Harvard, seven newborn prehistoric spiders that have been frozen in a block of ice thaw out and escape into the countryside. They begin spinning their webs in a tree under which seven little girls are having a club meeting. Each spider adopts one of the girls as a mother figure. When one of the girls' classmates discovers the spiders in a tangle of webs and chooses one to take to school for Show and Tell, she has no idea of the consequences that lie ahead. The spiders, an ancient breed of tarantula known as the Siberian snow spider, happen to have a poisonous bite. As the threat of the spiders grows, the true hero of the story is Miss Earth, beloved teacher at the Josiah Fawcett Elementary School, who risks her life for her students.

———. *Six Haunted Hairdos*. Illus. Elaine Clayton. New York: Clarion, 1997. (Middle Reading)

This follow-up to the successful *Seven Spiders Spinning* (1994) lacks the suspense that makes the first book deliciously scary. Thekla Mustard, president of the girls' club Tattletales, is still the confident feisty leader she always has been, but her confidence is shaken when maverick Pearl Hotchkiss joins with the boys to turn the tables on Thekla, who has frightened the boys by having the Tattletales dress up as ghosts. The ghosts in this story, even the real ones, just don't have the substance to be a real threat, and when everything finally comes together— Thekla's girls join with the boys to defuse the situation—the story lacks the drama of the first book.

Nolan, Han. *Dancing on the Edge*. San Diego: Harcourt Brace, 1997. (Young Adult)

Miracle McCloy finds it extremely difficult to live up to her name. She sees herself as a nonperson, fading into nothingness. Miracle was taken from her mother's body after her mother died in an accident, an event that she finds embarrassing and somewhat obscene, and her father, a brilliant writer who became famous at the age of 13, leaves her when she is 10. Her clairvoyant and mystical grandmother denies that he left of his own accord, saying that he "melted." As Miracle struggles to come to terms with her strange life, her inability to fit in at school, and her lack of identity, she is severely burned when she lights candles to invoke her missing father and is consequently institutionalized. Her relationship with her psychiatrist, Dr. DeAngelis, allows her to confront the truth about herself and her family and to finally accept herself without shame.

Willner-Pardo, Gina. *Daphne Eloise Slater, Who's Tall for Her Age.* Illus. Glo Coalson. New York: Clarion, 1997. (Early Reading)

Daphne is constantly harassed by Leonard DiMaggio, who calls her "giraffe" and makes her the brunt of jokes in her third-grade class. Her grandmother notices how quickly Daphne is growing out of her blue jeans, and Daphne begins to feel self-conscious about how tall she is. It doesn't help that her grandmother, at 5'8', is also tall for her age. In science class, Daphne's favorite, she is paired with Leonard and discovers something about him that he would prefer she didn't tell others about. She keeps his secret and gains his respect, and even though he doesn't stop teasing her, a connection develops between the two of them that wasn't there before.

APPENDIX A:
BIBLIOGRAPHY OF
RECOMMENDED
BOOKS FOR GIRLS
AND BOYS

Each group of titles below explores or promotes a character trait that can lead to mature thinking for both girls and boys. Brief descriptions of the individual titles can be found on the Internet at http://www.amazon.com.

1. Cleverness	8. Personal Values
2. Confidence	9. Resourcefulness
3. Courage	10. Responsibility
4. Creativity	11. Self-Reliance
5. Determination	12. Sense of Identity
6. Independence	13. Sensitivity
7. Logic	14. Spontaneity

CLEVERNESS

Adler, David. *Cam Jansen and the Chocolate Fudge Mystery.* Illus. Susanna Natti. New York: Puffin, 1993. (Middle Reading)

Emberley, Michael. *Ruby.* Boston: Little, Brown, 1990. (Early Reading)

Friedman, Aileen. *The King's Commissioners.* Illus. Susan Guevara. New York: Scholastic, 1994. (Early Reading)

Hooks, William H. *The Three Little Pigs and the Fox: An Appalachian Tale.* New York: Simon & Schuster, 1997. (Early Reading)

Yolen, Jane. *The Ballad of the Pirate Queens.* Illus. David Shannon. San Diego: Harcourt Brace, 1995. (Middle Reading)

———. *The Emperor and the Kite.* Illus. Ed Young. New York: World Publishing, 1967; New York: Putnam, 1988. (Early Reading)

CONFIDENCE

Cleary, Beverly. *Ramona the Pest.* Illus. Louis Darling. New York: William Morrow, 1968. (Middle Reading)

Cole, Joanna. *The Magic School Bus* series. Illus. Bruce Degen. New York: Scholastic, 1986–1998. (Middle Reading)

Duvoisin, Roger. *Petunia.* New York: Knopf, 1950. Reprinted in Duvoisin's *Petunia the Silly Goose Stories.* New York: Knopf, 1987. (Early Reading)

Enderle, Judith Ross, and Stephanie Gordon Tessler. *Nell Nugget and the Cow Caper.* Illus. Paul Yalowitz. New York: Simon & Schuster, 1996. (Early Reading)

Fenner, Carol. *Yolanda's Genius.* New York: Simon & Schuster, 1995. (Middle Reading)

Gauch, Patricia Lee. *Christina Katerina and the Box.* Illus. Doris Burn. New York: Coward, McCann, 1971. (Early Reading)

Kiser, SuAnn. *The Hog Call to End All!* Illus. John Steven Gurney. New York: Orchard, 1994. (Early Reading)

Lindgren, Astrid. *Pippi Goes on Board.* Trans. Florence Lamborn. New York: Viking, 1957; New York: Puffin, 1977. (Early Reading)

———. *Pippi in the South Seas.* Trans. Gerry Bothmer. New York: Viking, 1959; New York: Puffin, 1977. (Early Reading)

———. *Pippi Longstocking.* Trans. Florence Lamborn. New York: Viking, 1950; New York: Puffin, 1988. (Early Reading)

Lovelace, Maud Hart. *Betsy and Tacy Go Downtown.* Illus. Lois Lenski. New York: Thomas H. Crowell, 1943; New York: Harper, 1993. (Early Reading)

———. *Betsy and Tacy Go over the Big Hill.* Illus. Lois Lenski. New York: Thomas H. Crowell, 1942; New York: Harper, 1993. (Early Reading)

———. *Betsy-Tacy.* Illus. Lois Lenski. New York: Thomas H. Crowell, 1940; New York: Harper, 1993. (Early Reading)

———. *Betsy-Tacy and Tib.* Illus. Lois Lenski. New York: Thomas H. Crowell, 1941; New York: Harper, 1993. (Early Reading)

McPhail, David. *Annie and Company.* New York: Holt, 1991. (Nursery/Preschool)

Maguire, Gregory. *Seven Spiders Spinning.* Illus. Dirk Zimmer. New York: Clarion Books, 1994. (Middle Reading)

Meddaugh, Susan. *Martha Speaks.* Boston: Houghton Mifflin, 1994. (Early Reading)

Pfeffer, Susan Beth. *Sara Kate, Superkid.* Illus. Suzanne Hankins. New York: Holt, 1994. (Middle Reading)

Sendak, Maurice. *Maurice Sendak's Really Rosie Starring the Nutshell Kids.* New York: Harper, 1975. (Early Reading)

Taylor, Mildred. *Roll of Thunder, Hear My Cry.* New York: Dial, 1976. NEWBERY MEDAL. (Middle Reading)

COURAGE

Blegvad, Lenore. *Anna Banana and Me.* Illus. Erik Blegvad. New York: Aladdin, 1985. (Early Reading)

Brink, Carol Ryrie. *Caddie Woodlawn.* New York: Macmillan, 1935;

New York: Aladdin, 1990. NEWBERY MEDAL. (Middle Reading)

Choi, Sook Nyul. *Year of Impossible Goodbyes.* Boston: Houghton Mifflin, 1991. (Middle Reading)

Frank, Anne. *Anne Frank: The Diary of a Young Girl.* New York: Doubleday, 1952; New York: Bantam, 1993. (Middle Reading)

George, Jean Craighead. *Julie of the Wolves.* Illus. John Schoenherr. New York: Harper, 1972, 1974. NEWBERY MEDAL. (Young Adult)

Henkes, Kevin. *Chester's Way.* New York: Greenwillow, 1988. (Early Reading)

Jeram, Anita. *Daisy Dare.* Boston: Candlewick, 1995. (Early Reading)

Krause, Ute. *Nora and the Great Bear.* New York: Bantam Doubleday Dell, 1989. (Early Reading)

Le Guin, Ursula K. *A Ride on the Red Mare's Back.* Illus. Julie Downing. New York: Orchard, 1992. (Early Reading)

Pattou, Edith. *Hero's Song.* San Diego: Harcourt, Brace, 1991, 1998. (Young Adult)

Watkins, Yoko Kawishima. *So Far From the Bamboo Grove.* New York: Lothrop, Lee & Shepard, 1986. (Young Adult)

Zettner, Pat. *The Shadow Warrior.* New York: Atheneum, 1990. (Young Adult)

CREATIVITY

Bjork, Christina. *Linnea's Almanac.* Illus. Lena Anderson. Trans. Joan Sandin. Stockholm: R&S Books, 1989. (Middle Reading)

Brooks, Polly. *Queen Eleanor: Independent Spirit of the Medieval World.* New York: HarperCollins, 1986. (Middle Reading)

Christelow, Eileen. *What Do Authors Do?* New York: Clarion, 1995. (Early Reading)

Fitzhugh, Louise. *Harriet the Spy.* New York: Harper, 1964, 1990. (Middle Reading)

Konigsburg, E. L. *A Proud Taste for Scarlet and Miniver.* New York: Atheneum, 1973; New York: Yearling, 1985. (Middle Reading)

Kovacs, Deborah, and James Preller. *Meet the Authors and Illustrators: 60 Creators of Favorite Children's Books Talk About Their Work.* New York: Scholastic, 1991. (Young Adult)

Le Guin, Ursula. *Very Far Away from Anywhere Else.* New York: Atheneum, 1976. (Young Adult)

McClerran, Alice. *Roxaboxen.* Illus. Barbara Cooney. New York: Lothrop, Lee, & Shepard, 1991. (Early Reading)

Walsh, Ellen Stoll. *Hop Jump*. San Diego: Harcourt Brace, 1993. (Early Reading)

Wood, Audrey, and Don Wood. *Bright and Early Thursday Evening: A Tangled Tale*. San Diego: Harcourt Brace, 1996. (Young Adult)

DETERMINATION

Baum, L. Frank. *The Wonderful Wizard of Oz*. Illus. W. W. Denslow. Chicago: George M. Hill, 1900; New York: New American Library, 1984. (Middle Reading)

Booth, Barbara D. *Mandy*. Illus. Jim LaMarche. New York: Lothrop, Lee, & Shepard, 1991. (Early Reading)

Brown, Marc. *D. W. Flips!* Boston: Little, Brown, 1987. (Early Reading)

———. *D. W. Rides Again!* Boston: Little, Brown, 1993. (Early Reading)

Brusca, Maria Cristina. *On the Pampas*. New York: Holt, 1991. (Early Reading)

Dalkey, Kara. *The Heavenward Path*. San Diego: Harcourt Brace, 1998. (Middle Reading)

———. *Little Sister*. San Diego: Harcourt, Brace, 1996. (Middle Reading)

Danziger, Paula. *The Pistachio Prescription*. New York: Dell, 1978. (Middle Reading)

Greene, Bette. *Them That Glitter and Them That Don't*. New York: Knopf, 1983. (Young Adult)

Grimes, Nikki. *Meet Danitra Brown*. Illus. Floyd Cooper. New York: Lothrop, Lee, & Shepard, 1994. (Early Reading)

Hoffman, Mary. *Amazing Grace*. Illus. Caroline Binch. New York: Bantam Doubleday Dell, 1991. (Early Reading)

Konigsburg, E. L. *The View from Saturday*. New York: Atheneum, 1996. NEWBERY MEDAL. (Young Adult)

McCully, Emily Arnold. *Mirette on the High Wire*. New York: Putnam, 1992. CALDECOTT MEDAL. (Early Reading)

———. *Popcorn at the Palace*. San Diego: Harcourt Brace, 1997. (Early Reading)

Nolan, Han. *Dancing on the Edge*. San Diego: Harcourt Brace, 1997. (Young Adult)

Pomerantz, Charlotte. *The Outside Dog*. Illus. Jennifer Plecas. New York: Harper, 1993. (Early Reading)

Roop, Peter, and Connie Roop. *Keep the Lights Burning, Abbie.* Illus. Peter E. Hanson, 1985; Minneapolis, Minn.: Carolrhoda, 1987. (Early Reading)

INDEPENDENCE

Bosse, Malcolm. *Deep Dream of the Rain Forest.* New York: Farrar, Straus & Giroux, 1993. (Young Adult)

Cole, Babette. *Princess Smartypants.* New York: Putnam, 1987. (Early Reading)

Gauch, Patricia Lee. *Christina Katerina and the Time She Quit the Family.* Illus. Elsie Primavera. New York: Coward, McCann, 1987. (Early Reading)

Henkes, Kevin. *Sheila Rae, the Brave.* New York: Greenwillow, 1987. (Early Reading)

Jeram, Anita. *Contrary Mary.* Boston: Candlewick, 1995. (Early Reading)

Keene, Carolyn [Stratemeyer Syndicate]. *The Secret of the Old Clock.* New York: Grosset and Dunlap, 1930; Bedford, Mass.: Applewood, 1991 (rev.). (Middle Reading)

Keller, Holly. *Geraldine's Blanket.* New York: Greenwillow, 1984, 1988.

Lindgren, Astrid. *Ronia, the Robber's Daughter.* Trans. Patricia Crompton. New York: Viking, 1983; New York: Puffin, 1985. (Middle Reading)

Merrill, Jean. *The Girl Who Loved Caterpillars.* Illus. Floyd Cooper. New York: Philomel, 1992. (Early Reading)

Tripp, Valerie. *Happy Birthday, Samantha! A Springtime Story.* New York: Scholastic, 1991. (Early Reading)

Tusa, Tricia. *Stay Away from the Junkyard!* New York: Simon & Schuster, 1992. (Nursery/Preschool)

LOGIC

Carroll, Lewis [Charles Dodgson]. *Alice's Adventures in Wonderland.* Illus. John Tenniel. London: Macmillan, 1865; New York: St. Martin's Press, 1977. (Young Adult)

Crowley, Michael. *Shack and Back.* Illus. Abby Carter. Boston: Little, Brown, 1993. (Early Reading)

Meddaugh, Susan. *Beast*. Boston: Houghton Mifflin, 1981. (Nursery/Preschool)

PERSONAL VALUES

Cooney, Barbara. *Miss Rumphius*. New York: Penguin, 1982. (Early Reading)

Hamilton, Virginia. *Arilla Sun Down*. New York: Macmillan, 1976; New York: Scholastic, 1995. (Young Adult)

Klein, Norma. *Mom, the Wolf Man, and Me*. New York: Pantheon, 1972. (Middle Reading)

Nolan, Han. *If I Should Die Before I Wake*. San Diego: Harcourt Brace, 1994. (Young Adult)

Paterson, Katherine. *The Great Gilly Hopkins*. New York: Crowell, 1978. (Middle Reading)

RESOURCEFULNESS

Blumberg, Rhoda. *Bloomers!* Illus. Mary Morgan. New York: Simon & Schuster, 1993. (Early Reading)

Chandra, Deborah. *Miss Mabel's Table*. Illus. Max Grover. San Diego: Harcourt Brace, 1994. (Early Reading)

Cushman, Karen. *The Midwife's Apprentice*. New York: Clarion, 1995. NEWBERY MEDAL. (Middle Reading)

Gauch, Patricia Lee. *This Time, Tempe Wick?* Illus. Margot Tomes. New York: Coward, McCann, 1974. (Middle Reading)

Hamilton, Virginia. *Her Stories: African American Folktales, Fairy Tales, and True Tales*. Illus. Leo Dillon and Diane Dillon. New York: Blue Sky Press, 1995. (Middle Reading)

Hopkinson, Deborah. *Sweet Clara and the Freedom Quilt*. Illus. James E. Ransome. New York: Knopf, 1993. (Middle Reading)

Konigsburg, E. L. *From the Mixed-Up Files of Mrs. Basil E. Frankweiler*. New York: Atheneum, 1967; New York: Buccaneer Books, 1992. NEWBERY MEDAL. (Middle Reading)

Minahan, John A. *Abigail's Drum*. Illus. Robert Quackenbush. New York: Pippin, 1995. (Middle Reading)

O'Dell, Scott. *Island of the Blue Dolphins*. Boston: Houghton Mifflin, 1960; New York: Yearling, 1987. NEWBERY MEDAL. (Middle Reading)

Riggio, Anita. *Beware the Brindlebeast*. Honesdale, Penn.: Boyd's Mills Press, 1994. (Early Reading)

Saul, Carol P. *Someplace Else*. Illus. Barry Root. New York: Simon & Schuster, 1995. (Nursery/Preschool)

Schields, Gretchen. *The Water Shell*. San Diego: Harcourt Brace, 1995. (Early Reading)

Turner, Ann. *Dakota Dugout*. Illus. Ronald Himler. New York: Macmillan, 1985. (Middle Reading)

RESPONSIBILITY

Adler, Susan S. *Samantha Learns a Lesson: A School Story*. New York: Scholastic, 1986. (Early Reading)

Buss, Fran Leeper. *Journey of the Sparrows*. With Daisy Cubias. New York: Penguin, 1991. (Young Adult)

Byars, Betsy. *The Summer of the Swans*. New York: Viking, 1970; New York: Puffin, 1996. NEWBERY MEDAL. (Middle Reading)

Gates, Doris. *Blue Willow*. New York: Viking, 1940; New York: Puffin, 1976. (Middle Reading)

Haas, Irene. *The Maggie B.* New York: Aladdin, 1975. (Early Reading)

Hoban, Russell. *A Birthday for Frances*. Illus. Lillian Hoban. New York: Harper, 1968. (Early Reading)

Johnston, Tony. *Day of the Dead*. Illus. Jeanette Winter. San Diego: Harcourt Brace, 1997. (Early Reading)

Lasky, Kathryn. *Beyond the Burning Time*. New York: Blue Sky Press, 1994. (Young Adult)

McCully, Emily. *Mirette on the High Wire*. New York: G.P. Putnam's Sons, 1992. CALDECOTT MEDAL. (Early Reading)

McKinley, Robin. *The Hero and the Crown*. New York: Greenwillow, 1984. NEWBERY MEDAL. (Middle Reading)

MacLachlan, Patricia. *Sarah, Plain and Tall*. New York: Harper, 1985. NEWBERY MEDAL. (Middle Reading)

Paterson, Katherine. *Lyddie*. New York: Lodestar, 1991. (Young Adult)

Sendak, Maurice. *Outside Over There*. New York: Harper, 1981. (Middle Reading)

Temple, Frances. *Taste of Salt: A Story of Modern Haiti*. New York: HarperCollins, 1992. (Young Adult)

Turner, Ann. *Elfsong*. San Diego: Harcourt, Brace, 1995. (Early Reading)

Wilder, Laura Ingalls. *Little House in the Big Woods*. New York: Harper, 1932, 1993. (Early Reading)

Yolen, Jane. *The Devil's Arithmetic*. New York: Viking, 1988. (Young Adult)

SELF-RELIANCE

Bingham, Mindy. *Minou*. Illus. Itoko Maeno. Santa Barbara, Calif.: Advocacy Press, 1987. (Early Reading)

Block, Francesca Lia. *Weetzie Bat*. New York: Harper, 1989. (Young Adult)

———. *Witch Baby*. New York: HarperCollins, 1991.

Bunting, Eve. *Train to Somewhere*. Illus. Ronald Himler. New York: Clarion Books, 1996. (Middle Reading)

Burnett, Frances Hodgson. *A Little Princess*. Philadelphia: Lippincott, 1905; New York: Dell Yearling, 1975. (Middle Elementary)

———. *The Secret Garden*. Philadelphia: Lippincott, 1911; New York: Random House, 1993. (Middle Reading)

Cowen-Fletcher, Jane. *Mama Zooms*. New York: Scholastic, 1993. (Early Reading)

Creech, Sharon. *Walk Two Moons*. New York: HarperCollins, 1994. NEWBERY MEDAL. (Young Adult)

Field, Rachel. *Hitty: Her First Hundred Years*. Illus. Dorothy Lathrop. New York: Macmillan, 1929; New York: Yearling, 1990. NEWBERY MEDAL. (Middle Reading)

Frank, Lucy. *I Am an Artichoke*. New York: Bantam Doubleday Dell, 1995. (Middle Reading)

Hooks, William H. *The Girl Who Could Fly*. Illus. Kees de Kiefte. New York: Simon & Schuster, 1995. (Middle Reading)

Lord, Betty Bao. *In the Year of the Boar and Jackie Robinson*. New York: Harper, 1984, 1986. (Middle Reading)

MacLachlan, Patricia. *The Facts and Fictions of Minna Pratt*. New York: HarperCollins, 1988, 1990. (Middle Reading)

Maguire, Gregory. *Missing Sisters*. Dublin: The O'Brien Press, 1994; New York: Hyperion, 1998. (Young Adult)

Oneal, Zibby. *A Long Way to Go*. Illus. Michael Dooling. New York: Penguin, 1990. (Early Reading)

Schroeder, Alan. *Minty: A Story of Young Harriet Tubman*. Illus. Jerry Pinkney. New York: Bantam Doubleday Dell, 1996. (Middle Reading)

Speare, Elizabeth George. *The Witch of Blackbird Pond.* Boston: Houghton Mifflin, 1958. (Middle Reading)

Thompson, Kay. *Eloise.* Illus. Hilary Knight. New York: Simon & Schuster, 1955. (Early Reading)

Wersba, Barbara. *Tunes for a Small Harmonica.* New York: Harper, 1976. (Young Adult)

Wisniewski, David. *Elfwyn's Saga.* New York: Lothrop, 1990. (Early Reading)

SENSE OF IDENTITY

Anonymous. *Go Ask Alice.* Englewood Cliffs, N.J.: Prentice-Hall, 1971; New York: Aladdin, 1998. (Young Adult)

Babbitt, Lucy Cullyford. *Where the Truth Lies.* New York: Orchard Books, 1993. (Young Adult)

Baum, L. Frank. *The Marvelous Land of Oz.* Illus. John R. Neill. Chicago: Reilly and Britton, 1904; New York: Dover, 1969. (Middle Reading)

Blume, Judy. *Are You There, God? It's Me, Margaret.* New York: Bradbury Press, 1970; New York: Laurel Leaf, 1991. (Middle Reading)

———. *Deenie.* New York: Bradbury, 1973; New York: Laurel Leaf, 1991. (Middle Reading)

Bunting, Eve. *I Am the Mummy Heb-Nefert.* Illus. David Christiana. San Diego: Harcourt Brace, 1997. (Early Reading)

Carlson, Nancy. *Louanne Pig in Making the Team.* Minneapolis, Minn.: Carolrhoda Books, 1985. (Early Reading)

Choi, Soon Nyul. *Halmoni and the Picnic.* Illus. Karen M. Dugan. Boston: Houghton Mifflin, 1993. (Early Reading)

Cristaldi, Kathryn. *Baseball Ballerina.* Illus. Abby Carter. New York: Random House, 1992. (Early Reading)

Donoghue, Emma. *Kissing the Witch: Old Tales in New Skins.* New York: HarperCollins, Joanna Cotler Books, 1997. (Young Adult)

Fox, Mem. *Whoever You Are.* Illus. Leslie Staub. San Diego: Harcourt Brace, 1997. (Early Reading)

Garden, Nancy. *Annie On My Mind.* New York: Farrar, Straus & Giroux, 1982. (Young Adult)

Garland, Sherry. *The Last Rainmaker.* San Diego: Harcourt Brace, 1997. (Young Adult)

Gripe, Maria. *Agnes Cecelia.* Trans. Rika Lesser. New York: HarperCollins, 1991. (Middle Reading)

Hamilton, Virginia. *Zeely.* New York: Macmillan, 1967; New York: Aladdin, 1993. (Middle Elementary)

Kindl, Patrice. *Owl in Love.* Boston: Houghton Mifflin, 1993. (Young Adult)

————. *The Woman in the Wall.* Boston: Houghton Mifflin, 1997. (Young Adult)

Le Guin, Ursula K. *Tehanu: The Last Book of Earthsea.* New York: Atheneum, 1990. (Young Adult)

L'Engle, Madeleine. *A Wrinkle in Time.* New York: Farrar, Straus & Giroux, 1962; NEWBERY MEDAL. New York: Dell, 1976. (Middle Reading)

Newman, Leslea. *Heather Has Two Mommies.* Illus. Diana Souza. Northampton, Mass.: In Other Words Publishing, 1989. (Early Reading)

Philip, Neil, and Nicoletta Simborowski, trans. *The Complete Fairy Tales of Charles Perrault.* Illus. Sally Holmes. New York: Clarion, 1993. (Middle Reading)

Rathmann, Peggy. *Ruby the Copycat.* New York: Scholastic, 1991. (Early Reading)

Staples, Suzanne Fisher. *Shabanu.* New York: Alfred A. Knopf, 1989. (Young Adult)

Willner-Pardo, Gina. *Daphne Eloise Slater, Who's Tall for Her Age.* Illus. Glo Coalson. New York: Clarion, 1997. (Early Reading)

SENSITIVITY

Byars, Betsy. *The Pinballs.* New York: Harper, 1977, 1993 (Middle Reading)

Goble, Paul. *Beyond the Ridge.* New York: Bradbury Press, 1989. (Early Reading)

Hendrick, Mary Jean. *If Anything Ever Goes Wrong at the Zoo.* Illus. Jane Dyer. San Diego: Harcourt Brace, 1993. (Early Reading)

Jukes, Mavis. *I'll See You in My Dreams.* Illus. Stacey Schuett. New York: Knopf, 1993. (Early Reading)

MacLachlan, Patricia. *Mama One, Mama Two.* Illus. Ruth Lercher Bornstein. New York: Harper, 1982. (Early Reading)

Mori, Kyoko. *Shizuko's Daughter.* New York: Henry Holt, 1993. (Young Adult)

SPONTANEITY

Alexander, Sally Hobart. *Maggie's Whopper.* Illus. Deborah Kogan Ray. New York: Simon & Schuster, 1992. (Early Reading)

Henkes, Kevin. *Julius, The Baby of the World.* New York: Greenwillow, 1990. (Early Reading)

Lotz, Karen E. *Can't Sit Still.* Illus. Colleen Browning. New York: Dutton, 1993. (Early Reading)

McKissack, Patricia C. *Mirandy and Brother Wind.* Illus. Jerry Pinkney. New York: Knopf, 1988. (Early Reading)

Montgomery, Lucy Maud. *Anne of Green Gables.* Boston: L.C. Page, 1908; New York: Scholastic, 1989. (Middle Reading)

In addition to the above titles, the following list consists of female protagonists who can be respected as role models.

Bober, Natalie S. *Abigail Adams: Witness to a Revolution.* New York: Atheneum, 1995. (Middle Reading)

Greene, Carol. *Elizabeth Blackwell: First Woman Doctor.* Danbury, Conn.: Children's Press, 1991. (Middle Reading)

Hong, Lily Toy. *The Empress and the Silkworm.* New York: Albert Whitman, 1995. (Early Reading)

Kidd, Nina. *June Mountain Secret.* New York: Harper, 1991. (Early Reading)

Lee, Jeanne M. *The Song of Mu Lan.* New York: Front Street, 1995. (Early Reading)

McCully, Emily. *The Bobbin Girl.* New York: Bantam Doubleday Dell, 1996. (Middle Reading)

Miller, William. *Zora Hurston and the Chinaberry Tree.* Illus. Cornelius Van Wright and Ying-Hwa Hu. New York: Lee & Low, 1994. (Middle Reading)

Moss, Lloyd. *Zin! Zin!! Zin! A Violin.* Illus. Marjorie Pricemen. New York: Simon & Schuster, 1995. (Early Reading)

Nash, Ogden. *The Adventures of Isabel.* Illus. James Marshall. Boston: Little, Brown, 1991. (Early Reading)

Pinkney, Brian. *JoJo's Flying Side Kick.* New York: Simon & Schuster, 1995. (Nursery/Preschool)

San Souci, Robert D. *Kate Shelley: Bound for Legend.* Illus. Max Ginsburg. New York: Bantam Doubleday Dell, 1995. (Middle Reading)

Sasso, Sandy Eisenberg. *But God Remembered: Stories of Women from Creation to the Promised Land.* Illus. Bethanne Andersen. Woodstock, Vt.: Jewish Lights, 1995. (Middle Reading)

Sisulu, Elinor Batezat. *The Day Gogo Went to Vote: South Africa, 1994.* Boston: Little, Brown, 1996. (Early Reading)

APPENDIX B:
RESEARCH
BIBLIOGRAPHY

BOOKS ABOUT CHILDREN'S LITERATURE

Allen, Marjorie N. *100 Years of Children's Books in America: Decade by Decade.* New York: Facts On File, 1996.

Cameron, Eleanor. *The Seed and the Vison: On the Writing and Appreciation of Children's Books.* New York: Dutton, 1993.

Carpenter, Humphrey. *Secret Gardens: The Golden Age of Children's Literature from Alice in Wonderland to Winnie the Pooh.* Boston: Houghton Mifflin, 1985.

Cott, Jonathan. *Pipers at the Gates of Dawn: The Wisdom of Children's Literature.* New York: McGraw-Hill, 1985.

Hearne, Betsy, and Roger Sutton, eds. *Evaluating Children's Books: A Critical Look.* Champaign: University of Illinois at Urbana-Champaign, Graduate School of Library and Information Science, 1993.

Lipson, Eden Ross. *Parent's Guide to the Best Books for Children.* New York: Times Books, 1988.

Lynch-Brown, Carol, and Carl M. Tomlinson. *Essentials of Children's Literature.* Boston: Allyn & Bacon, 1993.

Plunkett-Powell, Karen. *The Nancy Drew Scrapbook.* New York: St. Martin's Press, 1993.

Rudman, Masha Kabakow, ed. *Children's Literature: Resource for the Classroom.* 2d ed. Norwood, Mass.: Christopher-Gordon Publishers, 1993.

Silvey, Anita, ed. *Children's Books and Their Creators: An Invitation to the Feast of Twentieth-Century Children's Literature.* Boston: Houghton Mifflin, 1995.

Trelease, Jim. *The Read-Aloud Handbook.* New York: Penguin, 1982.

BOOKS ABOUT FEMINIST THEORY

Aburdene, Patricia, and John Naisbitt. *Megatrends for Women: From Liberation to Leadership.* Rev. ed. New York: Fawcett Books, 1993.

Bingham, Mindy, and Sandy Stryker. *Things Will Be Different for My Daughter: A Practical Guide to Building Her Self-Esteem and Self-Reliance.* New York: Penguin, 1995.

Gilligan, Carol. *In a Different Voice: Psychological Theory and Women's Development.* Cambridge, Mass.: Harvard University Press, 1993.

Gilligan, Carol, Nona P. Lyons, and Trudy J. Hanmer, eds. *Making Connections.* Cambridge, Mass.: Harvard University Press, 1990.

Mann, Judy. *The Difference: Growing Up Female in America.* New York: Warner Books, 1994.

Phillips, Angela. *Discrimination: Past and Present.* New York: New Discovery Books, 1993.

Pipher, Mary. *Reviving Ophelia: Saving the Selves of Adolescent Girls.* New York: Ballantine Books, 1994.

Rappaport, Doreen, ed. *American Women: Their Lives in Their Words.* New York: HarperCollins, 1990.

Rosenman, Ellen Bayuk. *A Room of One's Own: Women Writers and the Politics of Creativity.* New York: Twayne Publishers, 1995.

Rutter, Virginia Beane. *Celebrating Girls: Nurturing and Empowering Our Daughters.* Berkeley, Calif.: Conari Press, 1996.

Sherr, Lynn. *Failure Is Impossible.* New York: Times Books, 1995.

Taylor, Jill McLean, Carol Gilligan, and Amy M. Sullivan. *Between Voice and Silence: Women and Girls, Race and Relationship.* Cambridge, Mass.: Belknap Press, 1996.

Wells, Diana, comp. *Getting There: The Movement Toward Gender Equality.* New York: Carroll & Graf Publishers/Richard Gallen, 1994.

Wolf, Naomi. *Fire with Fire: The New Female Power and How It Will Change the 21st Century.* New York: Random House, 1993.

ADDITIONAL BIBLIOGRAPHIES OF RECOMMENDED BOOKS FOR GIRLS

Bauermeister, Erica, and Holly Smith. *Let's Hear It for Girls: 375 Great Books for Readers 2–14.* New York: Penguin, 1997.

Odean, Kathleen. *Great Books for Girls.* New York: Ballantine, 1997.

INDEX

Boldface locators indicate extensive treatment of a topic. *Italic numbers* indicate illustrations with captions. An entry followed by an asterisk (*) denotes illustrator only. An entry followed by a double asterisk (**) denotes translator.

| T |